Advance Praise for
SMILING ON THE OUTSIDE

"What Ann does in this book, is what we as therapists dream our clients will do in a lifetime of sessions. She says with compassion for herself, what most want to hide - and hide from."

—Dr. Theo Tsaousides,
Author of *Brainblocks: Overcoming the 7 Hidden Barriers to Success*

"With courageous raw self-examination and astounding awareness, Ann has thrown wide the locked chamber of her silent, secret life, giving us hope for living in Joy with true and lasting transformation."

—Bob Wakitsch,
Co-Author of *The Midas Touch*

"*Smiling on the Outside* is captivating. Ann has a very powerful voice and I celebrate her courage to share her stories so others can know they are not alone."

—Ann Aubitz,
Author of *The Many Faces of Down Syndrome*

"*Smiling on the Outside* is a beautiful journey of truth, unabashed self-discovery, and introspective exploration of what it means to say the words, "I AM." The ease with which Peck shares her story and provides nuggets of wisdom that you can sink your emotional and intellectual wisdom into, gives readers the room to breathe into their truth, through the inspiration of honest, transparent, storytelling. As the saying goes, "Your truth shall set you free..." as will learning to smile on the inside."

—Rick Clemons,
Motivational Speaker and Author of
Frankly My Dear I'm Gay

"She's written this book for all of us who say, "Me, too" when reading her words, giving us permission to stop hiding our shame."

—Lisa Van Ahn,
Author of *I AM...A Girl's Guide to Harnessing Super Powers*

SMILING ON THE OUTSIDE

Secrets, Sex, Shame and the Search for Self-Love

Ann Peck

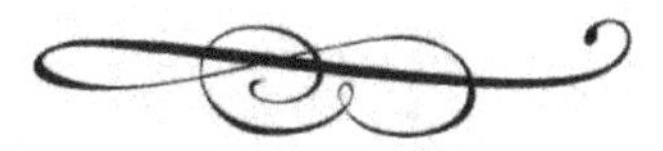

Curvy World Media

ISBN: 978-0-9984455-3-3
Library of Congress Control Number: 2016961603

Printed in the United States of America
First Printing: 2017

21 20 19 18 17 5 4 3 2 1

Cover & Interior Design by FuzionPrint
Back cover photo credit – Amy Zellmer

Curvy World Media
4707 Hwy 61 N, Suite 211
White Bear Lake, MN 55110

This book is for YOU—

so that you know you're not alone, you're not the only one,

and you're not crazy either.

Smiling on the Outside:
Secrets, Sex, Shame and the Search for Self Love
is a work of nonfiction. It is my story, my experience.
It is my truth as I know it today.
Some names and identifying details have been changed
and some events compressed.

Table of Contents

Chapter 1

Reflections on a Half-Lived Life

There is no safety in silence.
– Ann Peck

There she was, hours from taking her final breath, agonizing with the pain of bone cancer, struggling to speak. My mother was still beating herself up for how she had lived her life, or rather, how she had failed to live during her life. Lying in bed, no longer interested in food or water, she called me close. "Real close," she said while signaling me to come closer with her finger. Sitting next to her, my face inches from hers, she spoke.

"I wish I would have done more with my life. I wish I would have followed my dreams. I was afraid, and I didn't even try. Sweetheart, don't let your dreams die inside you."

How did she know? I had denied it for so long, but she saw me, and at that moment I was forced to admit it. "Me, too, Mom," I said to myself while smiling on the outside. I was walking the same path she had taken—the path of keeping secrets, hiding my pain, doing whatever it took to keep the man in my life loving me—and to keep him from leaving me.

I have kept secrets, simply because I've been afraid, afraid of what other people would think of me, what they would say. Seeking the approval of others while hiding myself in plain sight, I've spent a lifetime beating myself up for my choices, just like my mother. All because I've been ashamed of who I believed I really was.

I've learned, however, that the bravest thing we can do is to allow people to see us in the light, especially when that light reveals our vulnerabilities. It's also one of the scariest things to do, which is why so many of us take so long to step out of the shadows or never allow ourselves to be seen at all.

My mom had spent her life believing she wasn't good enough; believing she couldn't do, be and have all that she dreamed of. She was a creative soul, an artist, and storyteller. She danced, played the piano, and used to draw the most beautiful pencil and charcoal images of birds and flowers. She had talents, yet she hid them from the world and then from me after I happened upon a few of her drawings. In her final years, she asked for charcoals and drawing paper, yet couldn't bring herself to use them.

My mom lived with major depression and anxiety since before I was born, and while she never talked about it, the impact was obvious, and it was compounded from living with a verbally and emotionally abusive man—my stepfather—for almost thirty years. She spent her life feeling empty and unfulfilled because she believed she didn't deserve a better lot in life. She bought into the crazy, negative stories she told herself, no doubt the result of her mental illness and the abuse she endured. She had dark secrets and big dreams, both of which she kept silent about until the very end. When facing imminent death at her final life crossroads, it was too late for her. She finally shared her secrets, while her dreams died with her.

But this story isn't about her, not really.

Those secrets we all keep tucked neatly away in the corners of our hearts, or in the pits of our stomach, those are the secrets we need to shine a light on if we ever want to live out our biggest dreams, our deepest desires, and experience the bliss of a life full of freedom, joy, and overflowing love. Those are the stories we need to share if we ever want to accept ourselves for the beautiful souls we are.

The secret stories we need to uproot and examine are those we are most ashamed of and embarrassed by—the stories we *know* others will judge us for. They're the stories we've convinced ourselves make us look crazy, or evil, or selfish, or depraved. These are the stories about sex, failed relationships, mental illness, codependency or addiction. They tell about the things we have done or not done, or had done to us, whatever it was.

My mom lived what we'd call a *"good enough"* life. The day she died, I sensed that I had been doing the very same thing. However, I was too afraid at that point, to look within myself. I wasn't ready to face my past, my choices, my beliefs, or myself.

Perhaps you're living the same way, too.

So often, over time, our biggest dreams, our deepest desires, are shoved so far away from our consciousness, we're not even sure what they are anymore. They get buried under *the should, the must, the someday*. They're hiding underneath all the secrets and shame.

It's easy to forget who we are. Somewhere along the line, our self-concept takes its first hit, and we buy into a story of shame, which leads to a further weakening. Pretty soon a cycle forms. We begin telling ourselves things that aren't true because we believe something someone else said. We lose our integrity. We become closed off from others, never telling them the truth, because if they knew our deal, they'd run away. So we learn to be quiet, and cagey. We learn to keep problems to ourselves, instead of reaching out to others and getting the much-needed help. This is when our self-esteem crumbles, and we go into hiding. When facing life at a crossroads, we choose, to our detriment, the easy, comfortable and safe path instead.

We cannot understand the impact these stories, these dirty little secrets, have had on us by keeping them buried inside. The most powerful thing we can do is to share them with others, because through sharing, we begin to see the pieces we failed to see—the words, motivations, and deeds we'd misinterpreted. Suddenly, we realize we are not alone in our pain, embarrassment, and loneliness. We can connect, not only with ourselves but also with others on a deep level, because when we share our secrets, we discover a community who understands us, because they, too, have been there. When we come out from hiding and own our past, we realize we are not crazy, and that our world won't end if someone knows us for whom we are. That world will, in fact, blossom with a beauty we never knew possible.

We must share our stories because, until we understand them, we won't have a chance to interrupt the self-destructive cycle they have brought about. When we feel bad about ourselves, we begin overeating, drinking, isolating ourselves, dating "bad boys," and using sex to inflict self-harm, so we can forget the stories that got us to this place. We punish ourselves, beat ourselves up, and talk to ourselves in ways we wouldn't speak to our worst enemy.

What are you telling yourself?

Two of the most powerful words in the English language are I AM, because what follows those two words, defines us. What follows I AM will seek you out and define your reality. The wrong I AM can keep you from your destiny and keep you from living the life you've dreamed of.

As my mom had believed she was unworthy, I believed I was unlovable. That was how I walked through life. I'm going to show you how I got there, to that place of darkness, ruled by secrets and shame.

I'm going to reveal the stories that perverted my self-concept. And I'm going to share what it took to change. I'm going to share what I've learned about myself, so you can better know you. And when you find yourself saying, "Me, too!" take note, because even if we have more days behind us than in front of us, we still have more living to do. The time is now, my friends.
There is *no safety in silence.*

You see… this story isn't really about me either.

Chapter 2

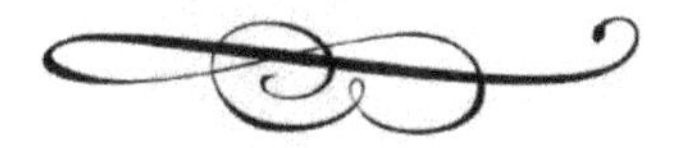

HIDING IN PLAIN SIGHT

When you start to feel like you don't matter,
you begin to act like you don't matter.
– Ann Peck

Most of us can identify the moment in time when everything began, when the first domino fell. For me, that moment was high school homecoming my senior year. I was eighteen. It was the final song before the dance ended when my former boyfriend asked me to dance. We'd been on-again-off-again sweethearts since the sixth grade, and a week before homecoming, he'd canceled our date in favor of taking a freshman to the dance. I pretended it was no big deal, but it hurt inside. We had broken up and gotten back together so many times before, yet the timing of this break up really threw me. It was our senior homecoming, I didn't have a date, and anyone who might have asked me had already asked someone else. I was stuck attending alone.

Worse, I was runner-up homecoming queen, elected by our school of 200 students, with no date/attendant by my side. Despite the classic Jackie Kennedy blue ball gown I wore, I was sure I looked pathetic. I'd watched him on the dance floor with the young girl, who didn't even look like she had entered puberty yet, and wondered what was wrong with me. I was tall, graceful, with curves in all the right places, and I was smart. Why would he have chosen her over me?

An hour later, he finally asked me to dance. As we swayed back and forth to the mellow lyrics of Air Supply, he whispered, "Have you ever done something you completely regret? I wish I wouldn't have broken our date. I wish we had come here together. I made a huge mistake."

I wanted him to beg me to forgive him, offer to take me home or out with our friends. Something. I wanted him to make up for everything, especially the fact that I had to endure the humiliation of attending this significant dance without a date. But once the song was over, he headed off the dance floor and disappeared.

After the dance, all of the couples headed out to the truck stop café or Happy Chef to grab a bite to eat. I changed out of my ball gown into jeans and headed over to a guy friend's house, where all of us without dates planned to hang out and drink, a usual Friday night activity in our rural community.

Only five of us made it out to my friend's farm. Usually, a much larger group of us hung out, twenty-plus, but as the rest of our friends were doing the date thing, we five were left to carry on the way we normally would.

Even though it was only the first weekend in October, the Iowa weather was already moving in, and we were grateful to be gathering inside a warm house, particularly one where the parents were not home. My friend's younger brother, a freshman in high school, was also entertaining three of his buddies, who were planning on staying over. They were out and about doing their own thing, while my four guy friends and I gathered at the kitchen table to drink whiskey and play cards. Drinking with the guys was my way of fitting in, belonging.

After a few hours and drinking way too much, it was evident none of us were in any condition to drive. One by one, we called our parents. The guys had it easy for they simply had to tell their folks they were staying over. As a girl, calling to say I was staying over at a boy's house was a little different, especially given my strict Catholic parents. They asked if the boy's parents were home, and even though they weren't home at the time, I figured they'd eventually show up, so I lied. "Yes, they're home."

I shouldn't have been surprised when they let me stay. They knew the family. This wasn't unusual since everyone knew everyone in our farming community. The truth is, they were no doubt relieved when I said his parents were home because they were probably too drunk themselves to come pick me up.

I don't remember my mother being much of a drinker until she married my stepfather when I was eleven.

She'd become a different person, doing things she would not have done before, to fit into the new life she had chosen for us. Friday nights at the Eagle's Club, Saturday nights at the Moose Lodge, dancing and drinking. Lots of drinking. I knew to steer clear of my mom on those nights unless I wanted to end up in an argument, whereas, drinking turned my usually short-fused and hot-tempered stepfather into a mild-mannered pussycat. I spoke with him when I called home that evening.

My friend showed me to his sister's room since she was sleeping over at a friend's house. He wished me a good night and shut the door when he left.

The room spun. I wanted to shut everything out: my parents, my former boyfriend, the horrible feeling in my head and stomach. I had no energy for anything other than flopping on the bed and throwing a quilt on top of me. In a moment, I was out.

The next thing I remember, the sun was shining through the window. As I began to wake up, I realized that the quilt I had thrown over myself was gone. My mind foggy, I tried to make sense of how my bra had become undone, and my underwear didn't feel quite right.

I couldn't breathe as my mind tried to figure out how I had ended up in such a state of undress.

Finally sitting up, I looked around and spotted the quilt. Had I thrown it off? Had I started undressing in the middle of the night? That had to be it, right? I must have gotten hot, or confused, or something. I must have messed with my clothes in my state of drunkenness and completely forgot. It must have been me.

Deep inside, however, a voice told me there was something more—that there had been someone else responsible for leaving me uncovered, vulnerable, and exposed.

I sat on the side of the bed for what seemed like forever, trying to make sense of it all. My mind was littered with thoughts of what might have happened while I was too drunk to know. I kept trying to push the thoughts away, get rid of the idea that I had been raped.

NO. It wasn't possible, yet it was. NO, I kept saying to myself as I tried to figure out who would have done such a thing. Weren't those guys my friends? Could someone have broken into the house?

I needed to get out of there.

I felt numb. I exited my body and floated above. I watched myself from outside myself as this girl, me, adjusted her panties, zipped up her pants and tried, unsuccessfully, to re-hook her bra.

Damn boobs. I'd developed early, and while I didn't have the largest breasts in our school, I was close. And I had everything else working for me, too. I was a cheerleader, tall, blonde, smart, and nice. Way, way too nice. I'd already developed the habit of taking responsibility for other people's actions, and discounting my feelings and needs, as most codependents and children of alcoholics do. Even with this situation. I couldn't remember what had happened and yet, I blamed myself for whatever it was. Maybe I hadn't been raped; maybe I'd said "*Yes*." But I couldn't remember any of it. Still, I must have agreed. My friends wouldn't have done that to me if I hadn't agreed, so it must be my fault.

When I got home, I called my best friend and told her what I feared had happened. She said she'd ask around. We lived in a small community, and you couldn't keep things like that a secret. We knew who was sleeping with whom, who had had an abortion, who smoked pot, who's mom was having an affair with a married man, we knew everything. When she called me back later that evening, her first words were, "Ann, I am so sorry," and I knew.

Turns out, when we all went to bed that night, my friend's younger brother and his freshman friends hadn't. All four of them had decided to take something they would never have received under normal circumstances.

Without actual details and no memory whatsoever, my mind went crazy. How had it happened, and what had happened? I imagined all four of them crowded around my prostate body, looking at me, daring each other to touch me. In my mind, they took turns fondling my breasts after the first boy undid my bra. When I didn't wake up, I imagined they proceeded to my pants, undoing them, pulling them down around my ankles. Did they put their mouths on me? Did they penetrate me with their hands, objects or, did they penetrate me with their penises?

Even writing these words makes the bile rise in my throat and my stomach queasy. And this is where things still feel crazy, some thirty years later.

One of the boys felt so guilty; he handed me a note in school the next week. Shortly after, he apologized to me in person. I responded by hitting him as hard as I could while standing on the sidewalk outside the entrance to our high school, as everyone watched.

My friends were supportive of me, but at the same time, they wanted the problem to go away. No one wanted to talk about what had happened, they all wanted to pretend nothing was amiss. When I hit the boy, they felt that should be the end, and we would all move on.

I was called into the principal's office shortly after hitting him. Even back then, violence was not tolerated. Well, at least it wasn't tolerated on school property.

I disclosed the whole story to the principal, who was not known for his compassion for females. Sitting across from him in his office, knowing my friends and schoolmates could see me through his windows, I gathered all the strength I had inside of me, and I named names. And the names I provided were connected–the son of a school board member, the son of a high school employee, the son of a prominent family in the community, and the son of a family known for causing trouble with the school. All these families had been in the community since before these boys were born, and long before I moved there.

I was an outsider. I'd come to this town in sixth grade when my mom married a local farmer who had kept to himself before gaining a new family. My dad wasn't part of this rural community either. Even though he only lived ten miles away, and was president of the nearby hospital, the status he carried in the big city did not transfer to my small town.

The principal listened to my story. He professed his regret for what I had gone through, and he gave me a detention. "What you've described as allegedly happening, did not occur on school property, so I have no authority to deal with it."

I no longer cared about being polite and respectful, as I always had. Enraged, I challenged him on the word *allegedly*. I reminded him of the note I'd received, of the boy's confession. I went into a full description of how I'd found myself the morning of the incident. "There is nothing alleged about any of this. It happened."

Whatever may or may not have happened, he proclaimed, didn't happen on school property. The fact that I'd hit someone on school property, an act that would normally require him to give me an expulsion, under the circumstances, would be let go with after-school detention.

And that was the end of that until I got home and had to explain the reason for the detention to my parents, who up until that point, had no idea what had happened.

When I told my mom and stepdad, shit hit the fan. They didn't know how to deal with what had happened to me. From the time they were married, my mom struggled with how to satisfy both her husband and her daughter. Ultimately, she learned to take her man's side to survive and thus, in his presence, she supported his position as I told the story of my rape. My friend's dad, whose farm we were at, had commented to my stepdad earlier that very day about how he "didn't know he was running a hotel." This made my stepdad look bad for not knowing the parents weren't actually home, so he wasn't able to respond to me in a compassionate way. Not that he would've. He was the stereotypical Irish Catholic farmer, hotheaded and stubborn as hell. I was grounded and no longer allowed to use the car. I was 18-years-old, multiple boys had raped me—and *I was grounded*. When I asked why, I was told the reason was that I had lied about my friend's parents being home.

I then went to dinner with my dad and his wife to tell them about what had happened. My mom and dad had divorced when I was seven, after a separation of a couple of years. And then, when I was eight-and-a-half, my father remarried and had an instant family that included five children, three of them teenagers. The teenagers lived with him, but I was never even invited to spend the night.

My dad and his wife lived ten miles from our farm, and by now, my three step-siblings had moved out of their home, so my dad and his wife lived alone in a house built for a family. I asked them to either help me get my own place to live or to let me live with them for the rest of my senior year. They said no to both, and I was crushed. I blamed my stepmother. I knew my dad couldn't, or wouldn't argue with her on something that would impact her, *but I was so hurt*. And I was royally pissed, although no one knew it, as I kept my rage and disappointment inside. My dad had lived with his wife and her children, and now after I'd gone through a life-altering experience, he refused to step in and help me. Both my parents abandoned me. Neither one of them could be bothered to step in and stand up for me, put me first. Instead, they both kowtowed to their spouses, and I was left to figure it out on my own.

Less than a month after the incident, I dropped out of the choir, resigned from cheerleading, withdrew from everything that had ever meant anything to me. Nothing mattered anymore. When I looked in the mirror, I could no longer see the pretty, smart, popular cheerleader. The girl looking back was fat, dumb and unworthy of being loved.

I didn't plan on being around for much longer. I thought about all kinds of ways to end my life. The shotgun we owned would be too challenging and messy, pills might not work, and alcohol and pills combined would probably only make me sick. I could jump off the railroad bridge over the river, but I was afraid of heights, so that left my car, which I now had use of again.

It was a Saturday night, and my parents were out dancing and drinking. I took the car and drove around with no real destination in mind. As the clock ticked closer to midnight, I knew my parents would arrive home soon and wonder where I was. I didn't care, and since this was way before cell phones, they would have no way of finding me. I was in such terrible pain, but I wanted them to hurt, too. They hadn't helped me when I needed them, and in my mind, they hadn't even tried. Instead, they punished me and betrayed me. All of them had.

I found myself driving south on Interstate 29, heading toward Omaha. The tears fell as my speed increased. I was the only car on this stretch of highway, and I believed if I were going fast enough and drove my car head-on into a bridge support, I would be dead before anyone happened upon me.

I could see the next bridge coming up and decided this would be it. Racing at 80, 85, 90, 100 and 110 mph, all I needed to do was point my car in the direction of the support, and it would all be over in a matter of seconds. I did, and at the last moment, I took my foot off the gas, righted my course, exited off the interstate and found a gravel road where I parked the car. I cried until the sun came up.

When I arrived home the next morning around seven or eight, my mom came running out of the house. She'd been up all night worrying about me. *Good, I thought.* She let me sleep all day and on Monday, she took me to see my doctor, who suggested admitting me to the hospital under a diagnosis of having mononucleosis. Even back then, no one wanted to deal with rape or depression. Mono was a safe diagnosis that allowed everyone to feel good, and to stay in denial about what was going on with me.

My mom thought I was depressed, but she didn't know how to help me, and I didn't know how to let her in. At this point in my life, I had already learned how to disengage and pull away whenever things got uncomfortable for me. Turns out that the doctor they sent to talk with me didn't know how to help me either. Even after sharing all of the details I knew about the rape and my feelings about myself, he told me if I didn't stop acting like a selfish brat and pull myself together, he would send me to the psych floor.

I was back home twenty-four hours later.

The experience drove home the message that keeping secrets from those close to me was necessary, and *that there is safety in silence.*

Returning to school marked the beginning of my hiding in plain sight.

Even though I had only been gone from school for a couple of weeks, and no one except a teacher I was close to knew what had happened, it was difficult returning.

There were so many questions from everyone, and I felt like a different person after everything that had happened. I no longer felt connected to the individuals who had been my closest friends, and I simply went through the motions of lunches at our group's table and after-school chitchat. I started moving away from my crowd and started hanging out with classmates who smoked pot, kids who didn't remind me of all I had lost. They didn't care about cheerleading, choir, or grades. They accepted me as I was, without question or judgment. Smoking pot with this group was my way of fitting in, belonging.

I met with the guidance counselor upon my return, and we spent hours planning for my future. I no longer wanted to be in school. I wanted to get my G.E.D. and go off to college. I wanted to get away, and he wanted to know why.

I shared the story of what had happened with my guidance counselor. By now, I was calling it a "sexual assault," a true enough account of the events, and a description I could say without wanting to vomit every time. He listened, professed his sorrow for what I had been through—but went right back to selling me on why staying in school was a good plan.

Even though I didn't know it at the time, both my principal and school counselor were classified as "mandatory reporters," which means they were obligated, by law, to report my disclosures to law enforcement. These two men were required to report my "sexual assault"—and they did nothing. Like everyone else around me, they didn't care about what had happened to me. They had no concept of the damage that had been done to my person, my confidence, and my very heart and soul. They only cared about appearances and their reputations. God forbid they would have acknowledged a student in this small school had been raped by four of their own. The scandal would have rocked our rural community, and clearly, to them, my health and wellbeing weren't worth it.

**I AM Worthless. I AM Weak. I AM Nothing.
I AM Unlovable.**

Reflections in the Rearview Mirror:

Sharing my rape story, and then getting those negative reactions from my parents and the authority figures involved, taught me to shut up, shut down, and go within.

Those who were supposed to love, protect, and support me, instead abandoned, betrayed and ignored me. Sadly, it happens in this world all the time.

Every day we read about girls who have been raped, and the crime is ignored. When the sexual violation involves alcohol, it's even easier to blame the victim. She learns to blame herself. It's your fault, we tell ourselves, so keep your mouth shut. There is safety in silence, we believe. Deal with it yourself; it's easier that way.

You will start to feel like you don't matter:

- If you don't reach out for help.
- If you don't keep trying.
- If you don't acknowledge what happened.
- If you don't do what you need to do to heal.
- If you don't work on feeling okay about yourself, loving yourself.

What are your "Me, too! Moments" from this section?

Visit www.AnnPeck.com/Me-Too or text ME-TOO to 44-222 to receive your free *Me, too! Moments Manifesto*

Chapter 3

WHEN THE BOUGH BREAKS

I'm here to tell you that hope is not a strategy,
and that fairness does not always win the day.
– Ann Peck

I left the farm a week after graduating from high school, spending the summer in my own apartment before moving into the college dorms. Still reeling from the aftereffects of the rape, my first college experience resulted in less-than-stellar grades. I wound up trying another school, a couple of different full-time jobs, and eventually landed at the school where I would finally earn my degrees. It was there I met the man who would become my husband and the father of my children. I was twenty-four when I met Jack.

By age thirty-six, Jack and I had been married for six long years, and together for ten. He was no longer employed, so he was always around, and I found myself more and more excited for my work trips, especially the ones requiring me to leave on a Monday and return on Friday. I was speaking for two different companies, my primary source of income came from presenting sales seminars and pitching a product from the stage, while the other was a sales training program. During this particular week, my main gig had me scheduled to give four seminars in Iowa, a different town each night. The locations weren't very exciting, yet I was looking forward to getting away from home. For the first time in a long time, I wasn't bringing the children with me.

These trips had turned into my escape. They were a time for me to live as the woman my audience perceived me to be: confident, successful, and free. I had it all, or at least they thought I did—a life created by design. I worked out of my home, had time with my children, and possessed the freedom to schedule my business around my home life, all while making more than enough money to support a household of four. I projected the image of living the life I'd told my audience was possible for them.

Each time I gave a seminar, I grew stronger. At home, however, I became weaker. I'd walk around on eggshells, script everything that came out of my mouth for fear I'd say something wrong, and I'd hide out in my home office whenever my husband was around. I lived in a constant state of anxiety and turmoil, yet I never told anyone. Except for work and our weekly homeschooling group, I was completely isolated. Girlfriends were non-existent in my life.

Jack and I had been fighting more than ever. The already touchy situation was aggravated by the fact that

I'd had four weeks off during the holidays, and only recently returned to work. It seems that the more time we spent together, the more conflict arose.

The children and I never knew who we were going to get when Jack came into a room. Would he be happy, or angry and demanding? Would we do something wrong, say something wrong, or be in the wrong place at the wrong time? Figuring out the right words to use when communicating with him was exhausting. I'd think through multiple possible scenarios before I dared open my mouth. Our eight-year-old daughter was a spitfire and unpredictable. He'd been browbeating me for years, and now he was going after her. Because she refused to measure her words, she always set off her father. Stepping in between the two of them was something I had to constantly be prepared to do. Our son was three-years-old at this time, and seemingly unaffected by what was happening in our home. His father regarded him as a prized child, much as his older half-brother had been. Jack didn't show the same love and respect to females as he did to the males in his family.

Reality hit me hard when, while I was traveling for work, my daughter called to say her dad was hurting her. It wasn't physical, but it was painful. Harsh words and being ignored are painful for all of us, and devastating for a child. That was the turning point, the moment I knew I had not been shielding my children. I hadn't seen it when I was at home, probably because I was in my own kind of survival mode. Being away, however, and feeling stronger on my own, I heard her words, and while they ripped my heart, they also gave me an absolute strength I would carry with me back into the home.

More reality greeted me upon my return home. Jack has used my computer in my absence, and now I found a trail of pornography websites in the computer's history, which might have gone unnoticed, were it not for the pop-ups and automatic dialers littering my screen. As I checked my computer's cookies and studied the history, I realized Jack had been spending hours every evening looking at these websites. These were hours when he should have been caring for our children.

My exposure to porn at that time was limited to "Playboy Magazine," courtesy of Jack. We had never looked at online porn together, nor had we discussed it. When I saw the title of one of the sites he'd visited: *Wife Swapping,* I became physically ill. Was he planning to force me to be with another man, I wondered? And then I found the photos he'd printed out from another site he'd visited. They were pictures of beautiful women—beautiful women who had penises. What was going on? What was wrong with me, I wondered? Had I done something, or not done something, to cause him to seek these things out? Nothing good could come of this I decided, and promptly called my doctor for an appointment.

Meeting with my doctor, I disclosed some of what had been going on at home. Failing miserably at my attempt to minimize the impact everything was having on the children and me, she gave me a diagnosis of anxiety and a referral to a psychologist. Jack was furious when he found out, telling me I should simply talk to him. I made a million excuses about why he couldn't help, yet he continued to push me to cancel my appointment. Finally, after making it clear the doctor believed it was necessary for my health, and telling him it was about my hormones or some such thing, he relented and agreed to let me go, while simultaneously punishing me with the silent treatment.

Jack had been sleeping in the downstairs family room for the last nine months, and it was taking its toll on everyone. He snored loudly, which gave both of us an excuse for him to sleep elsewhere without actually discussing what was going on—like how our marriage wasn't working. He consistently threw it back at the kids and me, somehow implying that he was a martyr because he slept on the sofa while the rest of us slept in beds. Even the kids complained about how his snoring kept them awake, so they weren't offering up their beds either.

Things came to a head one evening while we sat downstairs watching television. I mentioned something about giving me back my credit card, one on which he was merely an authorized user, and he stormed out of the room. He returned a few minutes later with the credit card cut up into tiny pieces. "You want your fucking credit card, here you go." There was something about the look in his eyes—the rage and barely contained disdain they revealed—and the way his lips twisted as he yelled, as well as how violently he threw the bits of the card at me, all let me know I didn't have much time.

I contacted a divorce attorney the next day.

Now it was time for me to get the hell out, with my kids intact.

I didn't anticipate the battle I'd be facing, and I most certainly didn't predict how Jack would respond, despite the fact that *the writing was already on the wall*. I didn't (want to) see it. No one did. Well, no one in my corner, anyway. And I realize how crazy that sounds after everything that was going on, but at that time, I couldn't see the fog I was living in, and therefore, couldn't imagine the war he'd wage against me.

Sure, I knew he'd be angry that I had taken a decisive step to put an end to our obviously unhappy relationship, but I was in such denial about the gravity of our situation that I honestly believed we'd work through the divorce in a friendly manner.

Looking back, it's easy to see how the trauma of our marriage, on top of the unresolved post-traumatic stress disorder (PTSD) from the rape, had both impacted me. I was not of a clear mind when I'd filed for divorce, which, as it turned out, really hurt me in the long run. I'd believed his lies and the put-downs for years. Our life together had been characterized by my saying *sorry* for everything that happened, with me taking responsibility for all of his behaviors in an attempt to keep the peace. Every time he'd shove me, or grab me, leaving a mark that would remain visible for hours, I'd apologize for being in his way. When his anger sent our son running away from him and into the banister, resulting in a trip to Urgent Care, I made excuses to the doctor. When he threw toys, hitting our daughter, I merely repeated his words, "It was an accident," while comforting her.

Five days after I'd made my visit to the divorce attorney, I met Jack in a coffee shop and told him I wanted out of our marriage. As I pulled the divorce papers out of my purse, he informed me that he had no intention of taking the papers, and he walked out.

That night, he came into our bed for the first time in more than nine months. He climbed in, moved close and wrapped his arms around me, where they stayed all night.

I didn't move, and I didn't sleep. I laid frozen in fear, my mind racing with possibilities of what Jack might do to me. Would he rape me? Hurt me? Kill me? And then my thoughts would go to the children. What would he do to them? Would he harm them to punish me?

It took going to court to obtain a temporary order before he moved out. He claimed he wouldn't leave without an order because he wasn't going to "walk away" and give up his rights. The court listened to our arguments and gave me sole physical custody, including all education and medical decisions. This, no doubt, was a result of their father saying that our daughter did not need therapy to deal with what was going on, and… *she can talk to him if she needs to talk to someone.*

After he moved out, I still couldn't sleep through the night. My anxiety intensified, and I was filled with fear about what he might do. He owned many firearms, which only amplified my fears. He knew the position of our bed relative to the window, which was on the backside of the house. I imagined how he could shoot me through the window, and no one would know. Had he installed cameras? Listening devices? Tapped the phone? Nighttime was the worst.

Things felt safer during the day, yet I was constantly on edge. Even though I was given sole access to our house, while he lived in an apartment, I was afraid to make any changes, even for my own safety. Not once did I consider installing an alarm system. I was still afraid of doing something, anything, to set him off. I had been beaten down for so long; I didn't trust myself. I didn't believe in myself. When he had been in the house, I was able to gauge my responses based on his actions and reactions. With him gone, I was flying blind. Every decision seemed critical, even the simple ones like what to have for dinner.

I found my attorney through a woman's crisis center. When I'd told her my story, things seemed simple enough. She let me know how the court proceedings and custody case would go and gave me her assessment of what the result would look like. Her fees were inexpensive compared to the other options out there, and she even let me save money by coming into her office and doing some of the legwork myself, like photocopying, research, etc. Being involved gave me a sense of control over my life, while not wasting financial resources that could best be used for the children and me. Even though I was supporting our family with my speaking career, I knew things would become more challenging with two households.

A few months after Jack moved out of our home, my attorney and I were served with notice that Jack would be seeking full custody of our children, ages three and eight.

This made no sense to me.

How could Jack possibly believe he could get custody after everything he'd done? On top of that, I had been both the primary parent, and the principal wage earner. I'd worked about a hundred nights per year giving seminars, and even then, our children traveled with me most of the time. I'd been doing it all, yet he was claiming the children would be better off with him. It seemed insane and a complete waste of resources to go down this path, yet a part of me feared that everything he'd ever said about me *was true*. He could win.

My lawyer thought it ridiculous, merely an attempt at gaining leverage for a better financial settlement. She saw no way that he would win—everyone knows that mothers don't lose custody unless they are drug addicts, criminals, or plain crazy. I was none of those things.

I believed her, yet deep inside, I feared the possibility.

We went through mediation and a court-mandated custody evaluation, and when the report came back, the evaluator recommended custody to Jack, saying that domestic violence was not an issue in our marriage and that I would likely alienate the children from their father in the future if they remained in my custody. She went on to claim that he was the *"friendly parent,"* and the one most likely to ensure an ongoing relationship with the other parent.

Reading through the report, I didn't even recognize the person she portrayed as my children's father. Hell, if I had been married to the man she was describing, I never would have filed for divorce. I tried to make sense of everything. What had I missed? What did I do wrong? This woman spent an hour in my home and a couple of hours talking to our children and me, didn't she see me? And what had he done to her? How did he fool her into seeing him as someone no one knew? She claimed Jack was a victim and had witnessed physical violence between his own parents. He'd vowed that he would never do that to his wife or children. She described Jack as a kind, generous father who had been actively involved in the day-to-day caring for the children. The report also noted that the children had a closer relationship with their father than their mother, which didn't fit with my experience, and which I later came to understand are common in these sorts of cases.

I read through the report numerous times trying to comprehend what had happened. I felt nauseous, overwhelmed, and frantic to find a way to change it, to fix it. The horror of reading the words on the page, knowing that this one woman's opinion would form the basis for my children's foundation and future. One woman's opinion. I wanted to scream. I was panicked. Couldn't anyone else see how crazy all this was? What was going to happen to my babies, and how was I going to protect them now?

And then it happened. I experienced a full-blown panic attack.

It would take years before I understood the classic characteristics, how domestic violence, power, and control are systematically used in our legal system to manipulate outcomes. As outrageous as it seemed, and still seems today, my plight and that of my children was not uncommon. The pendulum has swung, and while it is still a firmly held belief that mothers always receive custody, the facts prove otherwise, although no one talks widely about these mothers' facts and the experiences. It's probably because mothers feel shame when their experiences of domestic violence, emotional abuse, and even sexual abuse of their children, is denied by the very authorities who are supposed to protect them. Reminiscent of what happened with my own rape, this is why long ago I adopted the false belief that *keeping traumatic events a secret was a good survival mechanism.*

Being a mother is a significant part of a woman's identity, so when a woman who isn't crazy, isn't a criminal, and who isn't abusive, loses custody of her children, her identity is stripped away in the most personal and intimate way imaginable. She feels alone with no one to talk to, because whenever she tries to speak of the injustice, even her closest friends and family want to know: "What aren't you telling us," and "How is this possible, you must be leaving something out." The more she tries to explain what happened, the crazier she feels, because she lived through it and can't make sense of it. How will she help others understand? Believing she can't, she shuts down, and feels *it really must be her*—something must be terribly wrong with her. She really must be unworthy of being a mother. She believes there is safety in silence.

My father stepped in and offered to pay for the services of an expert to work with our family to create a parenting plan that would be in the best interests of our children. Jack reluctantly conceded and, after months of working together, we finally came up with an acceptable plan. Our children would split their time equally between both homes. We'd also split expenses evenly, so no child support was necessary. He was self-employed and making a decent living, roughly equivalent to my income, which had gone down due to the stress of the divorce proceedings. We each agreed to the hashed-out plan and began the new schedule. Everyone believed it to be fair.

When it came time to sign the official document and submit it to the court, Jack refused. He stated he would not sign our agreed upon parenting plan until we had the financial settlement worked out and both documents were ready to be submitted to the court. There wasn't much to settle on the economic front, so we agreed to continue with the negotiations.

And that's when it happened.

I was served with papers.

Jack was seeking full custody as recommended by the evaluator, along with more than $1,200 per month in child support.

What the hell was going on? We had spent months creating and agreeing to a plan that served our children best—a plan *we agreed* was best for them. Why would he now argue our children would be better off living with him full-time? It had to be about the money, and about punishing me because it most certainly wasn't about our children. And what if the court agreed? How would I keep our house if I had to pay that much in child support? Where would we go? Where would they sleep, what about their friends? And what would people think of me if I weren't raising my children? What would my children think of me? Would they think I didn't love them anymore? Would they hate me? Every divorced mom I knew was the primary parent, even if the kids were splitting their time equally between households. What would it say about me if he got full custody?

My attorney continued to be optimistic, although not to the degree she had been previously. I began to doubt her ability, yet things had progressed too far to change mid-stream. I needed to believe that she'd win the battle, so things continued.

Negotiations stopped, and we prepared for trial.

On the first day of trial, the judge compelled us back to the negotiating table. The last offer from Jack and his attorney was to agree to the parenting plan we'd created together with the parenting consultant in exchange for a flat payment of $50,000 for the financial settlement. At that time, I didn't have $500, let alone $50,000. I declined the request and entered into what would turn out to be a three-day trial that stretched over the course of as many months.

It didn't take long for me to figure out that my attorney was no match for the one Jack had hired. While my lawyer was focused on a peaceful resolution in the best and long-term interests of my children, his was an egomaniac focused on winning, no matter who they destroyed in the process. Where my attorney was gentle, patient and relaxed, his was articulate and pointed in her questions, fully in attack mode.

When it was my turn to take the stand, I told my story. I answered the questions asked of me. I cried, I shook, and I nearly wet my pants after the judge chastised me for my need to go to the bathroom, thereby making him wait on our first day in court. Jack's attorney was brutal, using the same tactics Jack had used on me for years. She pushed me to the edge and had me doubting myself and everything that I knew to be true.

As part of the custody evaluation, we each had been ordered to take the Minnesota Multiphasic Personality Inventory (MMPI). Jack had to take the test twice due to "an attempt to manipulate the results" on his first go round, but his attorney focused on my results. She said that the MMPI showed me to be selfish; then she said I portrayed the ultimate act of selfishness by filing for divorce. Selfish. Jack had called me selfish during our first year of dating, telling me I was too selfish to be a (step) mom to either his children or children of my own and then he broke up with me. Those memories came flooding back as I sat on the stand answering her questions.

Even in the midst of a brutal trial, *I still wanted to be loved and felt unlovable. I wanted validation and felt none.*

In addition to my speaking business, after the separation I had started working with clients and giving workshops on Emotional Freedom Techniques (EFT), an energy healing modality. His attorney mocked me, the modality, my work, and had me demonstrate the technique to the court, only to constantly interrupt me with her condescending questions. By the time she was done questioning me, I was doubting myself, despite the fact I'd had many paying clients and led numerous successful workshops. She then brought up how our nine-year-old daughter had shaved off her eyebrows while at her father's home, and accused me of suggesting that it made Jack a bad parent. She asked me if I thought I might be overreacting to the fact that my daughter had accidentally killed her brother's hamster at her dad's home. I responded that the truth was, she had squeezed it to death, and no, I didn't think I was overreacting. She dismissed my response and told the court Jack had talked with our daughter, and everything was fine. She claimed I was trying to use this "meaningless" incident to make Jack sound like a bad father. She portrayed me as a paranoid, overreacting flake who dramatized everything—all examples of why I should not receive custody, she argued.

Hindsight makes it easy for me to see that I was deep in the throes of PTSD by the time we got to trial. Jack's attorney had subpoenaed my therapy records as part of her trial strategy and as a result, I stopped going to therapy. Once again, I needed support and had nowhere safe to turn and so, true to my pattern, I kept everything inside and went silent again.

Two years after I had divorce papers drawn up to create a peaceful and safe life for my children and me, the real waiting began.

The judge had ninety days to determine our fate, and he used every last one of those days. Being done with the trial brought a sense of relief, but the waiting made every day stressful. The wondering, the not knowing, created a nerve-wracking limbo. As the days ticked by, I resolved to accept whatever decision the court made concerning custody. I knew custody reversals were exceedingly rare, plus the prolonged court battle and the fighting were taking a toll on the children. I was clear-headed enough to recognize that if I didn't receive custody, the attempt to reverse the decision would be long, expensive and even more challenging than the one we'd been through. Despite my pragmatism, deep down inside I believed that justice would prevail and that life and the judge would be fair.

On the Friday morning before Memorial Day, my attorney called with the verdict: Jack had been given sole physical custody of our children. I would be allowed to see them four hours during the week and every other weekend. His reasoning was a cut and paste from the custody evaluator's report. The judge's order would go into effect immediately.

I spent the next seventy-two hours in fear that Jack would show up at any moment and take our children away, something he was now legally entitled to do. Instead of showing up, however, he remained silent. We didn't hear a word from him until Monday afternoon.

I didn't sleep that weekend. Adrenaline and high anxiety kept me going, and I spent every possible moment I could with the kids. At night, when I didn't sit by their beds watching them sleep, I laid on the floor outside their bedroom doors listening to them breathe.

I prayed. I asked for answers. What had I done wrong? Why were we being punished? Would the children be okay? How would they be okay? Should I have stayed? Had the divorce been an awful mistake? How would I protect them now? How had things gone so wrong?

I got away. I was able to save myself, but I couldn't keep my children. What kind of mother can't keep her own children? I did everything I could, but I must have missed something. What did I miss? How could I fix this?

In the two years since we'd been living in the house without Jack, the children and I had created an environment where calmness was the norm. There was no yelling or screaming, and temper tantrums were relegated to bedrooms when necessary, and we were kind to one another. We talked about how we were feeling, we ate meals at the table and said prayers together every night. We had created a routine everyone found comfort in, and now it was shattering.

The voices in my head wouldn't stop. I needed to find a way to make everything okay for my babies, but I couldn't think. All those things he used to say about me were coming back. Maybe I *was* too selfish to be a mom. Maybe I really *didn't* know what I was doing. Once again, I began to question everything about myself. Maybe he was right. Maybe the judge was right. I must be a bad person. I must not be worthy of being a mother.

My children, by then ages five and ten, had no idea what was going on. Our time together was now limited, and I needed to help them understand what was going to be happening. The new arrangement would be a significant change from anything they had known. They would be leaving their home and going to live in an apartment where only one of them would have their own room. They wouldn't see their friends. They wouldn't see their neighbors. More important, they wouldn't see their mom. Even with the prior arrangement of one week with me and one week with their dad, they still saw me every day as Jack would drop them off when he went to work. They had spent their whole lives being cared for primarily by their mom, and that was about to change, dramatically.

I did my best to explain the new situation to the children. They cried and screamed while I attempted to stay calm and let them know it would all be okay.

None of us believed me.

In my heart, I was certain they were afraid they wouldn't see me again, that out of cruelty, their dad would run off with them to punish me. I believed my daughter was scared of what it would be like to be with her dad all the time, to have no one to step in and buffer her father's anger.

I had failed them. They could only blame me for not doing enough to keep them with me.

Monday arrived. We finally heard from Jack. He would be picking them up at 5:00 pm. We had a few hours to get everything together. We all moved around the house, gathering items, as though preparing for a funeral, which, in effect, we were. Our family and our dream of a peaceful and safe life had died. We were in mourning. Our once joy-filled house was a sharp contrast from where the kids would now be living—a place where walking on eggshells and monitoring their every word would be necessary for their survival.

When Jack arrived, I helped the children load their things into their dad's vehicle, kissed them and hugged them, knowing our lives would never be the same. And as they pulled out of the driveway, my strength vanished, and I fell into a heap on the garage floor, sobbing uncontrollably and praying the concrete would swallow me up and take away the pain.

I AM a Bad Mom. I AM a Failure.

REFLECTIONS IN THE REARVIEW MIRROR:

When deciding to divorce, whether for the first or subsequent time, we ask what it means about us. We label ourselves a *loser*, particularly when we lack confidence and self-esteem. We decide that we have only a certain number of chances, no matter how bad the situation, and after that, we're like the often-married Elizabeth Taylor, and everyone laughs at us. So we hold on, stay silent about what's going on in our marriage, and we remain stuck, so people won't talk bad about us. By doing so, we don't have to identify with what a loser we are. We blame ourselves for getting into the situation in the first place. We made our bed, so now, we lie in it.

I stayed in my marriage longer than I should have and yet when it was all said and done, I questioned if I had done the right thing by leaving. My worst fears had come to light, and the system had failed my children and me.

I trusted the authorities—my attorney, the custody evaluator, the judge—to do right by us. I believed that someone else had my best interests at heart. I didn't trust myself to be the best advocate for my children and me. I turned that power over to strangers, and I was wrong. And even when I saw it all going to shit, I stuck it out with my attorney, maintained the course, and hoped everything would work out the way it should. I banked on fairness prevailing.

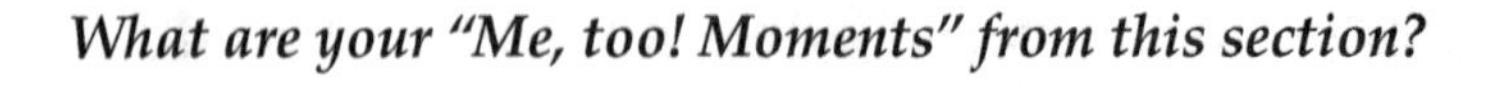

Visit www.AnnPeck.com/Me-Too or text ME-TOO to 44-222 to receive your free *Me, too! Moments Manifesto*

Chapter 4

WHEN THE FRIENDLY PARENT, ISN'T

We're on our own, more often than we'd like to think.
– Ann Peck

Summer vacation meant the children, and I spent a lot of time together after receiving the court ruling on custody. We didn't start experiencing the effects of the court-mandated schedule until fall when both kids were in school; my youngest having started kindergarten. It had been a little more than four months since the divorce was final.

Now, with no more weeks of vacation to look forward to, the transitions from my home back to Jack's were always tearful and rushed. The kids would take their time moving toward their dad's cargo van, and, not wanting to see them leave; I didn't exactly push them along either. Eventually, they would get settled into the van and be off until the next time we were to be together. This time, the visit ended much less peacefully.

My daughter was eleven and my son, a few weeks past six. As Jack loaded our son's bicycle into his work van, my little guy became hysterical, screaming and crying because, for some reason, he wanted to leave his bike at my house. The more Jack ignored him, the louder he screamed and the more both my daughter and I tried to soothe him. I was having a difficult time strapping him into his car seat in the back of the van. Nothing I did seemed to work.

Jack moved to the driver's seat, and my daughter buckled herself in, while I continued to talk to my son in an attempt to calm him down before he left. It had been important to me that the children didn't associate these transitions with too much drama, so I desperately wanted to soothe him, while knowing full well that Jack's patience was about gone. I could always tell by the way the energy in the space grew cold. And then there was the look. And the tone…always the tone.

"Leave him alone and get out of the van," Jack hollered over his shoulder. My daughter went silent in response.

"I'm still getting him strapped into his car seat," I replied without looking. Again, he hollered for me to get out of the van, and again, I replied our son was not yet buckled into his seat.

Moments later, Jack's patience wore out—and with the van's sliding side door open, our son still not strapped in completely, and me halfway inside the van—he put his foot on the accelerator.

The van rocketed forward. My body careened away from my son, without the row of seats found in standard vans to stop the momentum, my body smashed onto the floor of the vehicle. My one leg hung out, the only thing preventing the sliding door from closing. As quickly as he accelerated, he slammed on the brakes, sending me skittering across the floor of the van back toward my son who screamed in terror. My daughter shouted, "Dad, stop!"

"Get out of my van," Jack yelled again, and now, with both children terrified and screaming, I did the only thing I could think to do: I attempted to get up and reach my son. In response, Jack accelerated again and followed with an abrupt halt. Once again, I ricocheted across the floor. The children wailed.

In those precious seconds, as the children and I tried to make sense of what was happening, Jack got out of his seat and came around to the side of the van. He grabbed me, pulled me out of the vehicle, and threw me to the ground. I always knew it would come to this; the violence was always right below the surface, and now the monster was out.

As I struggled to get up and reach my distraught children, he yelled, clutched me by the arms, and shoved me back on the ground.

Everything happened so quickly. Neither of us spotted our daughter getting out of the van. She was now on her father's back, hitting him and attempting to pull him off me. She screamed in a voice more powerful than the strongest man. "**You don't hurt my mom!**"

"You don't hurt my mom!" Still, to this day, I have never heard such strength, such power as I heard in my little girl's voice that day.

Unable to get her father to stop, she ran into the house and came back out, phone in hand, and yelled, “I'm calling 911.” And she did. Through tears, she screamed into the phone, “Someone's trying to run over my mom.”

Those words still haunt me. Her father was trying to injure me in the van, he was throwing me to the ground outside the van, and he was trying to physically restrain me from rescuing my children. Suddenly, my children were witness to their father's rage against me. In seeing all this, the emotional response of an eleven-year-old went to what she imagined would happen next—and she took it upon herself to make sure it didn't.

It was then that her father released me from his clutches and ran to the driver’s side of the van, where he grabbed his cellphone and dialed 911.

My son was still partially strapped into his car seat, screaming hysterically, and in that split second, I had to make a choice. Do I go back in the van and attempt to rescue my son, or do I rush to my daughter, who is now standing in the garage on the phone? I was afraid of what might happen to my son if I ran to him with his father so near. Would he hurt me, hurt our son? Believing I didn't have time to get my son out of his seat; I ran to my daughter. She immediately handed me the phone, with the 911 operator on the other end.

The operator wanted to know if everyone was okay, if there were any weapons involved, and where everyone was located at that moment. She wanted to know if I felt safe. I didn't.

The police arrived within minutes, sending two cars as they often do for domestic violence occurrences. They took statements from everyone, except my son, who was too young and now being held firmly in his father's arms. Seeing the consistency between the statements given by my daughter and me, the officers retrieved my son, placed him in my arms, then took my former husband away in handcuffs.

Less than five months had passed since our divorce had been finalized. During the divorce process, the court had determined that domestic violence had *not* been an issue in our relationship. They had called Jack the "friendly parent." And here he was, being carted off to jail.

My emotions ran the gamut. I wanted to scream to the world, "See, I told you. I didn't make it up." And I wanted to run into my house and hide. He had been taken away, and I was terrified of what he'd do when he came back, and if I'd ever really be safe. The children had witnessed it all. How would I help them? What must they be feeling? How would they survive his return? Would they each be punished—my son for crying, and my daughter for calling 911? He was so unpredictable, even his time in jail didn't make me feel safe.

The events of that afternoon were surreal, and this was the biggest disturbance our little suburban community had seen in the eight years I'd lived there. On that sunny October afternoon, not a single neighbor was outside. Hiding away safely in their houses, our screams traveling through their open screen doors, they'd peered through their shades as the drama had unfolded. And in the days and weeks that followed, not a single person spoke to me about it. When I most needed support and to feel safe in my neighborhood, it was non-existent. I imagined the worst and realized no one was in my corner. With no one to help, and no one to protect me, I was on my own, and I was terrified once again.

Family court refused to get involved, even after an emergency plea to the judge. The judge's comment was, "Let criminal court handle it," and with that, the children went back to Jack's when he was released from jail. I did my best to be strong for the children, while worrying about what would happen to them when they were alone with their father. The criminal court offered to grant me an order for protection; however, they refused to give one for the children, which meant, if I accepted the order for myself, it would be difficult, if not impossible, to see my children, as they lived with their father.

I declined the order and spent many sleepless nights wondering what was happening to my children, and what was going to happen to me now that things had escalated.

Even with the documented event, the arrest record, and the trauma my children both experienced, nobody in a position to do anything seemed to care. My parents were supportive, yet they lived states away, along with most of my closest friends. I was alone.

Meanwhile, I was crazy with worry. The experience was fuel for my untreated anxiety. I'd read the reports and seen the statistics. Most violence happens during the first two years post-divorce. We saw it on the news all the time. Husband kills children and himself. Husband kills wife in front of children. Husband kills children in front of wife. Husband runs off with children, and wife never sees them again. I lived in a constant state of fear.

Now that his mindset and actions were no longer hidden behind the closed doors of our lives, I knew he didn't have anything to lose. I obsessed that he would harm them, or worse, to punish me. I also worried about what he might do to me, now that he'd been jailed for something for which he could only blame me. Before, however, when we were in the same house, I'd accept the responsibility and spend hours convincing him I was sorry. With the divorce and separate homes, that wasn't going to happen. As I moved through the house, I avoided standing in front of the windows and doors, and at night, I kept the lights dim, so my movements wouldn't be seen from outside. I didn't know what to do, or where to turn.

Both attorneys stepped-in right away and agreed we needed to have our parenting consultant draw up a plan for transitions with the children to avoid any interactions between the parents. He was required to park on the street in front of my house, and I was to do the same if I was dropping them off at his home. The impact on the children was noticeable every time we saw each other. They clung to me even harder when we were together and, when it came time to leave, my daughter begged her brother to stay quiet and move quickly, so as not to keep Jack waiting. They had fallen in line and were doing what they needed to do to protect each other, and me.

I had been unable to protect my children and now, they had assumed the role of protector over me, which made me feel like an even bigger failure as a mom.

I AM Alone. I AM Terrified. I AM Powerless.

REFLECTIONS IN THE REARVIEW MIRROR:

When we stay long enough in dysfunctional relationships—and we always stay too long—we learn to ride the roller coaster of our partner's moods, make excuses for his behavior, and blame ourselves for everything he does and says, and everything that happens as a result. We live by the mantra, "it's my fault," and we don't tell a soul what's really going on behind closed doors. We keep our secrets, we live with our shame, and we lie to ourselves until something happens that makes that impossible.

Often, that *something* takes the form of violence. It's hard to hide the truth where violence is resulting in police reports, arrests, and court dates.

The fact is, it's not hard to get yourself in a situation where you could be killed. Unpredictability, the kind we dance around for years on end, can take a nasty turn into something more ominous, if not lethal. I was one of the lucky ones.

We believe that people will witness outrageous behavior, and somehow step in and save us. Often, they don't. When even the authorities don't help, we blame ourselves and begin owning the "guilty-victim" thing. It's our fault, we think, and we're not worthy.

Of course, that sets us up to be prime targets for "being rescued." We're beyond vulnerable. We feel rejected by everyone and everything that is supposed to help, so if someone shows up to save us, he could be

Jack-the-Ripper on a Triceratops, and we'd let him in. And we'd hang on for dear life, no matter how messed up the ride was. We'd manufacture a sense of security, see only what we wanted to see and feel grateful that at least *we are no longer alone.*

What are your "Me, too! Moments" from this section?

Visit www.AnnPeck.com/Me-Too or text ME-TOO to 44-222 to receive your free *Me, too! Moments Manifesto*

Chapter 5

THE CINDERELLA MYTH

We attract what we believe we're worth.
– Ann Peck

Nearly three years after I had the divorce papers drawn up and a few weeks after my former husband had thrown me around in his van, Drew reached out to me again. We'd met nearly two months before, had a couple of fun dates, but I hadn't heard from him since, and hadn't expected to. He had, after all, informed me that my children's ages served as a red flag. His kids were all grown up, so a relationship with me wouldn't make sense, he said. I'd told him to figure it out, and apparently, he had.

After explaining what had happened before his sudden reappearance, I was convinced he'd disappear again. But he didn't. Drew became my knight in shining armor. I was extremely vulnerable, and he offered me almost everything I dreamed of. Yet, something important was missing—a deeper connection, the kind where you get below the surface of the physical and connect on a soul level, a spiritual level. I never discussed this with him, because I didn't want it to mean what I feared it might. And I didn't tell anyone else, either, lest they attempt to suggest he wasn't the one for me. But I knew. And every time we had sex, I'd pay close attention to see if the emptiness was still there, and it always was. I figured that empty space would get filled once we stopped having sex and started "making love." We needed more time together, more shared experiences, I'd tell myself. Maybe I needed to love him more, I decided. And instead of considering *how maybe I needed to love myself,* I focused on escaping the life I had been living, and I believed Drew was my ticket out.

After introducing him to my children, my young son said to me, "Now Drew can protect you." Ever since the van incident, my son had taken on the role of protecting his mom—much-too-large a role for a child of six. Yes, Drew would protect me, now. He would protect me—and my kids.

A little more than twelve months after privately declaring our love for one another, Drew and I were getting ready to board a flight bound for the island where we would publicly declare our love in the presence of Drew's business friends and colleagues.

As we boarded the plane, the flight attendant took my wedding gown and hung it in a special place while we found our seats and settled in for the long flight to the island of Bonaire. We were both still groggy by the time we arrived at our hotel. A long overnight flight cramped in coach seats didn't exactly make for a restful night. After an hour of waiting, we were finally in our room. We had a view of the ocean with a balcony for relaxing and playing cribbage. The room was dated, and the air-conditioner didn't work consistently; however, our pending nuptials made everything seem perfect.

The evening of our arrival, the business group we were traveling with hosted a welcome reception for all those in attendance. These were the people who would be witnessing our wedding in a few short days—no family, no friends from back home—only Drew's colleagues and their spouses.

After making our way to the government center, we prepared for our meeting with the official, the magistrate who would be officiating our wedding ceremony, and then we finally met the woman with the power to either deny our marriage or make it happen. Even after all the paperwork we had submitted, the personal interview could make or break all the plans we'd put in place.

Drew immediately gained her confidence, as he did so often with people we met. Drew had a big personality and a big presence, and while I literally fell under his charm, he could metaphorically bring other people to that place. Before I knew it, the three of us were laughing and saying our goodbyes until the ceremony. Driving away, we were both relieved to have met with her approval, even as we realized neither of us remembered her name. All Drew recalled was her tight, sexy black blouse and cleavage, which I'd come to accept was pretty typical for the kind of things he remembered about women.

With all the business of the wedding taken care of, we now had a couple of days to relax and enjoy the beauty of the island before our ceremony. We spent our mornings scuba diving, our afternoons on the beach, and our evenings dining with Drew's colleagues and playing cribbage on our balcony.

My parents weren't there to witness our wedding, but their words of love and encouragement were. Mom was thrilled Drew would be part of our family, and I knew she was impressed her baby girl was marrying a doctor. It was that old stereotype about doctors being the ultimate catch—the ones to provide a beautiful life with all the trappings of success. My dad liked Drew and was happy I had found someone who treated me well and with whom I shared not only fun adventures but also an intellectual connection. Dad was less impressed than Mom in the outward trappings of success and most concerned for my emotional happiness and well-being. After Drew and I had announced our engagement and upcoming wedding, Dad called to share some fatherly wisdom.

"All couples have disagreements, and even if you haven't had them yet, you will. Choose your battles carefully." And so I did, probably more so than my dad intended.

Even though our wedding wasn't until sunset, I skipped the morning dives and spent time on the beach instead. It was Valentine's Day, and my wedding day. I woke up to the sounds and smells of the ocean. Everything was wonderful because today I marry the man who believes I am beautiful, sexy, smart, and kind. I still don't see myself the way he sees me, but one day, with his continued love, I'm convinced I will.

I'll never forget the look of adoration in Drew's eyes when we placed the rings on each other's fingers; I was bursting with anticipation for the life I would now be sharing with this man who saw me in ways I hoped to one day see myself.

I AM Married. I AM Saved. I AM Safe.

Reflections in the Rearview Mirror:

When we don't believe we can do it on our own, when we don't love and trust ourselves, it's easy to become mesmerized by things, whether they be fabulous trips, big diamonds, beautiful houses, or titles, such as "Doctor." We fall for the Cinderella myth, complete with the knight in shining armor swooping in to relieve our suffering. He'll put a pretty dress on us, marry us, and take care of us forever, just like we'd always dreamed.

At my most vulnerable time, my knight showed up in the guise of a doctor, someone who would give me self-esteem, someone with money, someone who thought I was worth something.

But shiny armor can be blinding.

I ignored all of the obvious warning signs, as we do. I allowed myself to be bought. I got married in front of strangers, with no family or friends, and refused to acknowledge how sad it made me feel. As to the nagging feeling that something important was missing? I did what many of us do: I kept that secret tucked far away in the recesses of my soul, falsely believing it would disappear if I ignored it because I was willing, or so I thought, to pay the price. At the time, I had no idea how much that decision would ultimately cost me.

What are your "Me, too! Moments" from this section?

Visit www.AnnPeck.com/Me-Too or text ME-TOO to 44-222 to receive your free *Me, too! Moments Manifesto*

Chapter 6

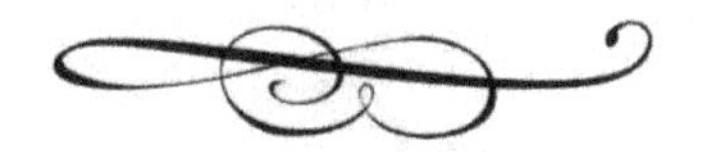

DROWNING IN THE SEA OF ADDICTION

Losing your identity and sense of self
is like sleep-walking through life.
– Ann Peck

Four months into our marriage, with the start of summer vacation, we experienced our first extended time with my children. Two full weeks together began the day school got out. We marked the occasion with a backyard pool party and barbecue, after cruising around with the top down.

A month later, Drew and I set off for what promised to be an adventure. It was the first trip to Europe for both of us, and I was thrilled to be sharing the experience with Drew. He'd traveled before we met, frequented all the warm places in the United States and throughout the Caribbean, which only made sense since he was nearly fourteen years older than me, and had the financial ability. The most exotic place I'd been up until that point was Hawaii with my dad and his wife, more than twenty years earlier.

We found ourselves walking the beautiful streets of Budapest, Hungary, and dining in an outdoor cafe serenaded by strolling musicians. Before meeting Drew, a dinner out meant eating at some place in the suburbs. I didn't drive a convertible; I drove a station wagon. I didn't visit Hungary; I visited Bismarck, North Dakota.

After a restful night's sleep, we boarded our cruise, which would take us down the Danube River. The boat was full, a hundred fifty passengers plus staff, and even though we were one of the last couples to sign up, I'd negotiated a fantastic deal on this cabin, and Drew agreed, it was too good to pass up. So we made our way to the largest upper deck cabin the ship offered. Heaven. *If my friends could see me now,* I remember thinking.

Numerous European riverboat cruises were available. The travel agents we'd used when going to Jamaica had sent us a promotional email, which we'd jumped on, not because of the route, but rather because it was a clothing-optional cruise. The idea of combining our love of being naked with a European adventure was extremely attractive.

Drew and I had discovered our inner nudists on our first trip to Jamaica, which, much like this trip, we booked specifically because of the option to be naked. Neither of us had ever tried the experience before, and we found ourselves loving it. Although, when we first arrived at the Jamaican resort, I was ready to bolt the moment I spotted a group of naked people playing bocce ball. It took a full day and lots of alcohol before I found myself comfortable enough to let go of all my inhibitions about letting strangers see me naked, and seeing them the same way. Being naked while outside and near the water turned out to be one of the most liberating and freeing experiences either of us had ever had, and we took every opportunity we could find to do that.

As we watched the guests boarding, both Drew and I sensed that this was going to be an adventure we'd not soon forget. From the scantily clad, over-tanned, tight-faced, nipped, tucked and abnormally perky-breasted women, to the bad dye jobs, golf-shirted and wandering-eyed men, the guest list was dominated by an over fifty and even sixty crowd trying to look younger. It was about as bad as your eighty year-old grandma going out in public wearing something from Forever 21.

We were only hours into the trip when we discovered we weren't on an actual clothing-optional cruise. The real amount of time we would be able to be naked on the deck of the boat was limited to times when we were cruising, and not even all the time, as some of the countries we would pass through had strict nudity laws.

The next day, while we were sitting on the deck, fully clothed, we got to know some of the other couples and learn how they came to be on the cruise. Both an American expat couple in their early fifties who lived in Italy and traveled the world, and a young couple from Miami in their early thirties, had come for "the experience." As the youngest people on the boat (I was the next youngest), the Miami couple seemed to be wondering whether or not "the experience" was going to be worth it. Lots of other couples had their own stories and reasons for being there. Some simply wanted to cruise Europe and take off their clothes. Others were trying to spice up their marriages, while others appeared mortified at the overt sexuality.

Drew and I were five months into our marriage, so this cruise was like another honeymoon for us. We spent time on deck playing cribbage and getting to know the other passengers.

Somewhere along the way, I earned the nickname "The Beauty Queen," which was used as a way to get our attention at dinner, or when we were off exploring the cities. The nickname made me extremely uncomfortable, as it drew people's attention my way, attention I was trying to avoid. The name had originated with a couple of women who had expressed their desire, as well as that of their husbands, in spending time with Drew and me—and not to play cribbage. Knowing they were having sexual thoughts about us, kept me on edge and looking over my shoulder. Drew assured me he wasn't interested, but I still couldn't fully relax.

Drew and I didn't follow the crowd when the boat docked, and we'd go off on our own to explore. It wasn't that the people weren't nice, most of them were extremely friendly, but we preferred to see the things you don't see when going with a tour group. I also needed the break from the energy of the group. The constant intensity and sexual tension made me uneasy and unable to relax without a cocktail or two, so sightseeing alone gave me time to regroup and connect with my husband in a way not possible on the boat. I wanted to see everything and capture it all in photos. We explored the river towns in Hungary, Germany, and Austria with my love beside me

As it turned out, only a few couples who, like us, had booked the cruise because it was clothing-optional. We learned from our shipmates that, because of the lack of interest and the empty cabins, the cruise was heavily marketed to *"the lifestyle"* community.

> *The Lifestyle: A community of consenting adults, where public or private sexual experiences may include self-expression, partner swapping, group sex, sexual touching, and voyeurism.*

Before we were married, when I still had my home and job, Drew and I had played around and tried a couple of these *lifestyle* experiences out of curiosity and a desire to add a new level of excitement to our sex life. We even discussed the idea of finding another couple who we could have a relationship with—sharing not only sex but an emotional connection. We talked about finding a couple with whom we could socialize, travel, and explore sexually. Our experiences, however, had always ended the same. Drew would be sexually satisfied, both from having encounters with another woman and from watching another man do the same to me. I would feel dirty, unfulfilled and empty inside, and I would end up "taking one for the team," as Drew would put it. I never told anyone what Drew and I were doing, *or how it made me feel.* Even though I went along with it in the beginning, it wasn't long until I felt uncomfortable and lost control of my own body and well-being. And even though Drew acknowledged these experiences weren't working for me, he always pushed for more.

Evenings on the boat became stressful as *The Beauty Queen* and her handsome husband received numerous offers to sit at various tables. Drew loved every minute of the attention, and I wanted to hide in our cabin, which of course, I didn't do. As a people pleaser, I found it difficult to disappoint others, even strangers. I wanted everyone to feel comfortable, have fun and relax, even if it meant I couldn't do any of those things. We'd made a significant investment to take this trip, and I wanted Drew to have a good time, too, so I forced myself to overcome my reluctance, and I showed up as a good sport.

In the bar, on the third night of the cruise, an attractive older woman befriended me. It started with her complimenting my dress, and then casually touching my bare shoulder. After a few more drinks between us, she pulled me onto the dance floor. It turned her husband on to see us rub against one another, dance provocatively, kiss and touch each other, even fully clothed. With enough alcohol flowing through my veins and the encouragement of my husband, I found this brief experience exciting, enjoyable and safe. A couple of minutes in, Drew stepped in to finish the dance as my partner. He was completely turned on from watching.

We left the dance, returned to our cabin and had sex. We also talked about my experience with the woman in the bar, and while it was enjoyable and exciting for both of us, it was nothing I wanted to repeat. Drew's words agreed, but I wasn't entirely convinced my little show with the woman had been enough to satisfy him.

On the fifth night of our cruise, we attended a big party in the boat's bar. Everyone was there. The music was loud, and the alcohol flowed. Drew and I danced and danced. We were having a fantastic time, as though we were the only two people there. Then Drew accepted an invitation from another woman to dance while we were enjoying a cocktail at our table. He suggested I give her husband a thrill by dancing with him. I opted out, and instead excused myself to the ladies room. When I returned, Drew continued to dance with a few other women and me, and I continued to decline invitations from their husbands, claiming the need for rest. The sexual tension of the group simmered below the surface, and by now, I was in full management mode, knowing where one false move on my part would lead us.

Drew liked being the center of attention, and with this crowd, it was like winning the lottery for him. While Drew danced with the other women, I tried to push the thoughts out of my head of where this could lead.

A few hours into the festivities, Drew came back from the men's room and invited me out to the deck to enjoy the beautiful evening. We stood on the deck, outside the doors to the lounge area, enjoying the quiet of the night, the water, and the twinkling lights of the city where we had docked. This was what I had been waiting for—a romantic, quiet moment alone with my husband, away from the noise and the lustful eyes of strangers.

Drew stood behind me and wrapped his arms around me as we gazed out over the water. I sank into him, breathing a sigh of relief and basking in the love we shared. Another couple soon joined us for the view, moving in without a word, engrossed in one another. They had invaded my private moment, and I wanted them to leave. I pulled Drew closer and stared off into the night sky.

Slowly, Drew partially withdrew from our embrace to put his arm around the other woman. He drew her close while continuing to hold me.

I suddenly realized that this couple's presence on the deck *was no accident*. Without warning, or time to make sense of what was happening, the woman was between Drew and me. First, they kissed. Then he began fondling her over and under her clothes. The music from the bar filtered out to us, and it combined with the sounds of the boat motors passing by, my husband's mouth sucking on the woman's skin, their moans, and her husband's groaning. The voices in my head began screaming for them to stop, to get me off the boat, to go back and erase everything. The noise was excruciating as I was emotionally raped by my husband, but I was unable to say a word or even move.

The only thing separating Drew and me was the woman. Our bodies all touched. Frozen in place, Drew didn't even see me. I felt non-existent as my husband's eyes came up from the woman's face and body and he looked right through me. He entered her from behind, and her head tilted back where it cradled next to his.

The rage and fear grew white hot inside me as my mind raced. *What if someone sees this? We could get in trouble, thrown in a foreign jail.* I was always worried about what other people would think of me, of us. How dare Drew do this? If someone saw what was happening, if we ended up in jail, our secret would be out, and that terrified me. Because once others knew our secrets, I'd be forced to acknowledge the truth of our relationship, and that frightened me more than anything.

Drew was in a sexual frenzy with her, his eyes looking straight at me, yet straight through me. My husband was having sex with a woman, easily in her sixties, and she was everything I was not.

Her husband was my height, older than her and he sported a comb-over. He stood next to me rubbing himself as he watched my husband with his wife.

I left my body and watched the events happening outside of me, same as I had done the morning after my rape when I was trying to make sense of what happened. And then I saw the expression I'd come to recognize. Drew's head tilted back, his eyes almost closed, his mouth opened, and his face contorted as though in pain. My husband moaned and climaxed with this stranger.

The couple left as Drew zipped up his pants. They exited as quickly and silently as they'd joined us.

Drew reached for me and pulled me close. I was still in shock. The whole thing was beyond bizarre, so different from any of our previous experiences with other people, where everyone knew each other, and nothing happened by surprise. Numb and silent, I tried to make sense of what had happened, but the noise both inside and outside my head was deafening.

"I don't understand why you're so upset. You were enjoying it." Drew said in response to my uncontrollable crying. We were now on the upper deck because I didn't want to walk back into the lounge as I was convinced that people had watched the whole thing. He seemed matter-of-fact. He smiled and nodded to get my agreement as he had done so many times before.

"Drew, what in the hell made you think I was enjoying that?"

"I was having fun, and you looked like you were having fun, Ann."

"How would you know? You didn't even notice me. I was frozen and couldn't move. My eyes were pleading for you to stop, and you didn't even see me."

I was beginning to understand it now. I wasn't entirely real and fully valued by my husband as a human being. He saw me as more of a thing, not a partner, and this terrified me. It was more than I could digest at the moment.

We made it back to our cabin without interacting with anybody else, and we went to bed without kissing each other goodnight, the first time we'd ever neglected that ritual. I was probably over-reacting. My thoughts raced through the whole gamut.

The next morning, I delayed getting ready to make sure we were late to breakfast, thereby avoiding most of our shipmates. We left the boat for a walkabout. Neither of us spoke of the previous night's events, although we both carried the energy of it with us. Ever since the rape, I'd become a pro at not talking about what was going on and keeping the pain inside, and while I believed I'd moved beyond that destructive way of being, this experience brought back my old behavior and beliefs: *Like, there was safety in silence, and keep my pain hidden and find a way to make everything okay, even if it didn't feel right on the inside.*

The stress finally took its toll, and my body responded quickly. By the time we returned to the boat a few hours later, I'd developed a fever and a sore throat. I encouraged Drew to attend dinner without me, not even caring what he would do in my absence. By the time he returned, my fever had spiked to 104, and I was delirious. Drew tracked down some medication and ice, and within a few hours, the fever broke. I wanted to take his loving attention as a sign he was remorseful and loved me, but something within me knew better.

I AM Trapped. I AM Invisible. I AM Heartbroken.

Reflections in the Rearview Mirror:

To handle what is happening to us, we ...

- Stick our heads in the sand like an ostrich, because we know if we admit that we know what's going on, we will have to do something about it.
- Ignore our mess because that's what we've always done.
- Think it will go away, or get better on its own.
- Delude ourselves because we stand to lose too much if we acknowledge the truth.
- Can't (or don't) come out and say something, even when our bodies beg for mercy by getting sick, experiencing pain, or shutting down. We don't (or can't) even make the connection on how these things are related to what's happening.

Five months into my marriage I saw my husband's sexual addiction for what it was. Financially dependent upon him, and with my whole identity and sense of worth tied up in being a doctor's wife, I was caught in the middle of it.

I was the doctor's wife with the big ring, the beautiful house, and all the trappings of success, proof that I had made it, and had escaped my former life. None of us want to admit we care about that material stuff, but we do. We hide behind our strong woman persona and pretend it doesn't matter, but it does. It matters so much that we're willing to do anything, even if it means selling our souls to keep from losing it because we equate having these things to being loved.

What are your "Me, too! Moments" from this section?

Visit www.AnnPeck.com/Me-Too or text ME-TOO to 44-222 to receive your free ***Me, too! Moments Manifesto***

Chapter 7

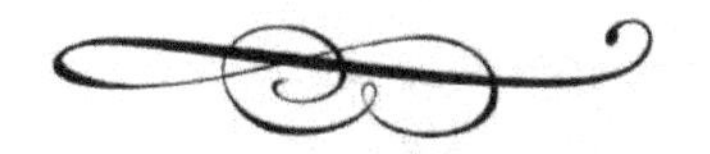

To Love, Honor, and Share

When you invest everything in someone else,
when you're shaky about who you are,
when you forget your power, your needs, your wants…
you wind up in an impossible situation.
– Ann Peck

Things between Drew and me were cool when we returned from our time in Europe. I refused to be intimate with him until he got a clean bill of health, and after spending weeks trying to convince me he didn't need one, and attempting to bribe me with shopping excursions for designer clothes and jewelry, he finally relented. With a negative test for sexually transmitted disease, and the September start of school for the kids, our lives returned to normal for a while.

Our version of normal included watching porn for Drew and his ongoing push to go back and try *the lifestyle* again. Before meeting Drew, I learned to enjoy some forms of porn on my own as I explored my sexuality. Once we became a couple, we shared our favorite videos and images with one another as a form of sexual foreplay. I don't recall when it changed; when Drew started viewing porn without me and I stopped looking at it entirely, except when we'd return to *the lifestyle* website where we'd connect with people we would consider meeting. The photos in people's profiles were similar to porn, and Drew would even sometimes masturbate while looking at them.

After months of Drew's insistence, I finally agreed to try *the lifestyle* again. He promised it would be different this time, yet getting ready for "dates" didn't feel different at all. I never knew what to wear, and would try on multiple outfits before finally settling on one Drew said looked sexy. I'd try on dresses, from all flowered to the tight, black sweater variety. I'd try on many skirts, each one getting shorter until they barely covered my butt. Then I tried on tops where the button-down blouses always bulged, and I knew Drew would tell me just to undo the button that was causing the problem, which made me extremely uncomfortable. The sweaters were low-cut and always tight. I hated seeing my "back fat" outlined by my bra strap. And Drew always suggested I go braless, because "I looked great." Surgery had made my breasts smaller, fuller, but not perky. In my mind, going without a bra and looking hot, was not a subsequent benefit from the surgery that Drew had paid for a mere six months into our dating relationship.

For Drew, it was always about me *looking hot.* Although, in hindsight, it was probably more accurate that Drew liked me to look slutty.

We were meeting the latest couple, a lawman and his wife, at a little place about twenty miles away from our home. Drew said we didn't want to risk running into people we knew, even though we were going to a place we had been many times before. I suggested this place because I felt safe there. It was familiar to me, and I felt more comfortable there than someplace I'd never been, especially since the other man worked in law enforcement. Simply by agreeing to meet them, I secretly felt as though we were about to go down the bottomless rabbit hole—and that I'd never get out. I was scared but didn't tell Drew. He would simply try to convince me that I was overreacting. Maybe I was. There was also a summer festival going on that evening, one that attracted people from all around the area, including the area where my kids were going to school. How was I going to explain being with this other couple if anyone saw us? You know how when you lose your virginity or get your period for the first time, you're convinced everyone can tell? It was like that. I was convinced anyone who saw the four of us would know we were planning to swap partners and then have sex.

I was nervous as usual. I was worried that I would shut down and not talk, which always made Drew angry. I was afraid Drew wouldn't stay next to me, and I'd be left on my own to deal with this other man. I was afraid Drew would become so focused on getting with this other woman that he'd forget I was there. I was scared it would be a repeat of past experiences where Drew would be fondling another woman under the table, or she would fondle him, all while the man would be attempting to do the same with me.

Drew kept telling me to relax and have fun, saying earlier, "I don't know why you're so worried. It's only dinner. Let's just go and have fun. If you're not comfortable, we'll leave."

I didn't dare start a fight as we were getting ready to go, but I knew…we never left these situations when I was uncomfortable. It was always the same. I'd get uncomfortable, and pinch Drew's leg over and over to get his attention. He'd cover my hand with his, pull me close and smile. But we'd never leave. Not ever.

He was working hard to convince me not to shut down and be quiet once the other couple arrived, and as always, I promised I'd do my best. "Once they get here, relax and be yourself. It will be fun. Shall I get you another martini? Would that help?"

We sat side by side in a booth away from the door. When the other couple arrived, there was the sort of awkwardness one would associate with being on a blind date, except we'd already seen naked photos of one another. That's the way it worked. No one ever wanted to meet without seeing what you looked like naked. Other couples usually only cared about what the woman looked like without clothes. In our online profile, we kept these particular photos locked, and gave the password only to people we were going to meet.

The lawman was over six feet tall, had light hair, healed-over pockmarks covered his face, and he had cold eyes. I now understood why he was either far away or wearing sunglasses in every photo they'd shared. She was the polar opposite of me, being petite, with dark hair and eyes, and small breasts. She was highly educated, as well as cute, toned and bubbly. Everything I wasn't, except for the higher degree. Unfortunately, even with a master's degree, I felt anything but smart as I looked at what my life had become.

Things started off as they always did with lots of small talk before moving into the standard questions regarding how long we'd been in *the lifestyle,* and what were we seeking.

No different than dating as a single person, you can pretty much count on someone saying something he or she thinks the other wants to hear. "You are even more beautiful in person." "You are so hot." "Your eyes are amazing." Everyone smiled and said thank you as the compliments were tossed around.

Drew had a habit of talking about me to other people as though I wasn't there. He'd say things about how I was nervous before we got together. Drew talked about how I was shy and needed time to get to know people to feel comfortable. He'd say things that I thought were private, and I'd pinch him to get him to stop. Sometimes it worked and sometimes it didn't. A few cocktails into the evening, the atmosphere became more relaxed. Drew told his usual jokes, everyone laughed, and I hadn't pinched his leg in at least twenty minutes.

And then it happened. Our food hadn't even arrived, and my husband suggested the men switch places. He always did this to me, saying something to the people we were with, knowing I wouldn't have the courage to say no and upset the dynamics. I had been going along with things for so long; he was aware that I wouldn't argue, especially not in a public place. So I smiled politely as the lawman sat down next to me, while Drew took the seat across from him, which made him too far away to pinch and too difficult to kick under the table. I was on my own, and I felt myself withering inside.

This was not how things were supposed to be. My life was not meant to be like this.

The lawman put his hand on my thigh and rubbed and squeezed every few minutes, while Drew felt up his wife under the table. I tried to pretend everything was normal and smiled and laughed at appropriate times. I enjoyed the teasing when Drew was next to me. I felt safe knowing I could smile or laugh in a flirty way, and the only hands that would touch me would be my husband's. But they weren't his hands on my thigh now, and I had to remind myself…

This was something I was doing to make my husband happy. Keep him happy. Keep him loving me. Keep him from leaving me.

The waitress came back to our table to check on our glasses and deliver our meals. I opted for another cocktail, and the men ended up sharing my plate of food as I claimed to be full from the bread.

Things felt much more comfortable when we left the restaurant, and we decided to walk over to the nearby summer's night festival. Drew walked with me at first, and then he suggested we walk hand in hand with each other's partner. I was feeling the effects of the cocktails and politely agreed. Being polite was my way of overcompensating. I agreed to Drew's suggestion, praying we wouldn't run into anyone we knew. I believed if anyone who knew me saw me holding hands with this man, I would be branded.

When the lawman asked if I wanted an ice cream, I jumped at the opportunity and requested a cup and spoon because you can't hold hands if you're eating with a spoon. Ice cream in hand, I felt much more relaxed and went on to enjoy the festival and getting to know our "new friends."

At the end of the evening, we parted ways and agreed to stay in touch. This was code for; we're going to talk as a couple and decide whether we're interested in having sex with you.

I never asked how other couples talked over such a possible liaison, but for Drew and me it was always the same. He enjoyed the women, thought they were cute or hot or sexy or whatever. Bottom line: He wanted to have sex with them. Years went by, and it finally dawned on me. Drew simply wanted to have sex, and he wasn't overly particular.

I would agree to go on another date to get to know them better first. I needed to have a connection. I needed to feel safe and cared about. I wanted my husband to care about me more than he cared about having sex with other women. And if I couldn't have that, I at least wanted the man I had to have sex with care about me.

We saw the lawman and his wife a couple more times. We went on their boat, hung out by our pool. Each time food was involved, and each time Drew and the wife were quick to get physical, which left me alone with the husband, who persistently pushed me to join in the fun. He tried all kinds of tactics including compliments, asking about my family, talking about Drew, and talking about how much he and his wife liked us. He was apparently trying to show me he cared about me, but his efforts were totally transparent. I didn't feel cared about at all; in fact, he scared me.

Within moments of sitting next to me on the side of our pool, he had untied the bottoms of my string bikini. Now mind you, I hadn't suggested he do so, nor had I given him any indication it was okay to do so. I suppose seeing my husband's mouth all over his wife's breasts made him feel entitled.

I needed a lot more alcohol to play the game, retied my bikini and suggested another cocktail. I was buying time, and he knew it. Something told me he wasn't going to be patient for long. All I wanted was for Drew to pay attention and realize what was happening—and ask these people to leave.

I made an excuse and walked away to get a towel and another drink.

After spending the afternoon at our pool, Drew had sex with the wife in our sunroom as the husband, and I watched. I was relieved Drew was getting his sexual fix as I believed it meant we'd be done soon. I was also terrified, as I knew this meant my turn was coming, and I wasn't sure I could pull off the whole "willing partner" thing.

And then it happened. The man made his move, and I had no way to get out of it without causing a major scene. My husband lay on the nearby sofa, masturbating while he watched. While the man forced intercourse, I watched from outside myself as he pumped away. I could see my face making all the right expressions, the moans coming out of me on cue.

This wasn't me; it was *her*—the same girl I'd watched dress herself after realizing she'd been raped.

When I'd married my knight in shining armor, I imagined a beautiful, normal life where we'd entertain, host dinner parties, and travel. I'd be involved in charity functions, do lunch with the ladies, get involved in the community and earn a name for myself in circles so far removed from my past life it would be as though it never existed. What I got was anything but normal. I had the beautiful house, as well as luxury cars, designer clothes, diamond jewelry, a full-length mink, and high-quality household furnishings. These things were nicer than any of the things I had previously enjoyed. It was hard for anyone to tell from the outside, looking in at all the beauty that surrounded me, that this wasn't a normal life.

Drew was anxious to get together with that couple again, even though I had told Drew about my experience of leaving my body and not feeling safe with Drew so far away. He suggested it would be better next time, and we should all be having sex at the same time, so Drew and I could be close, and I would feel safer. The next time I didn't feel safer, I simply went numb. I still left my body, viewing the scene from outside myself, looking down on the action. Because our four bodies were intertwined, I couldn't see *her*, so I closed my eyes from above and waited for it to be over, and at that moment, I would rejoin my body.

Things changed on my birthday. This couple was going to spend the night.

These people weren't close friends, and they weren't exactly lovers. We shared a secret, and the secret connected us. I didn't feel safe with this couple, or any of the ones that had come before, and at the same time, I enjoyed having other adults to talk with, do things with, and even flirt with. The flirting was fun and a turn-on.

This was a dangerous game. I was losing control. I was losing myself, and piece by piece, Ann was disappearing. I wanted to take my sexual excitement and share it with my husband, the two of us alone. My husband wanted sex with others, and to watch them have sex with me.

We'd spent the afternoon at the pool and grilled steaks for dinner. We'd had discussions about things moving fast, and everyone knew that *Ann needed more time.* No one was pushing me to get sexual, although, in the back of my mind, I knew I'd be expected to comply before the day was over. Drew already had sex with the wife, and when the husband would check in with me, I'd reply with a "not yet." The whole fantasy of getting aroused by watching other people during sex was lost on me now. I wasn't even jealous of this other woman anymore.

I was beginning, for the first time, to pay attention to myself, my own needs.

Toward the end of the evening, someone suggested we play cards—strip poker, of course.

During our card game, the three of them turned up the heat. It started out with a few comments tossed in here and there from our guests. They were wondering what they could do to make me more comfortable, and they offered all kinds of suggestions. "What if we all go up to your bed?" "How about we all take our clothes off and get into the hot tub together?" "Would you feel more comfortable if it were the two of you ladies, to begin with?"

I kept saying I didn't know and I needed more time.

I was struggling with old feelings of wanting to fit in, and being willing to do whatever was necessary to be one of the "cool" kids.

The pressure was intense, my insides were turning somersaults, but still I was feeling like the "party pooper." My mind was spinning with questions as to why my husband would even suggest I did this when he knew how it made me feel. I felt guilty for not going along with what Drew wanted, and I was scared what would happen if I didn't. The look of adoration I saw on our wedding day had long since disappeared, and I was sure if I stopped agreeing to these sorts of activities, Drew wouldn't want me anymore.

As Drew squeezed my upper arm, I realized the tone of the group changed. They were no longer patient, they were pushy, and I felt threatened. The lawman tried to make me feel guilty about the fact my husband had already had sex with his wife, and now it was his turn with me. There I was, in the house of my dreams, with all of my beautiful possessions surrounding me, this handsome man who'd married me and made it all possible sitting next to me, and I blurted out the words that changed everything, "I can't do this."

The three of them went into hyper drive suggesting ways, once again, to override my discomfort. I stayed firm, and then the wife got nasty. Maybe she worried about dealing with her husband if this didn't work out the way everyone else wanted. She'd already had sex with my husband; maybe that was going to be a problem for her if her husband didn't get to have sex with me. I don't know. She went off on how I had misled them into believing we liked them and wanted to have this relationship with them, and before she could say much more, her husband suggested that Drew and I talk through some things while he and his wife went upstairs to give us some space.

I knew Drew was disappointed in me. I could see it in his eyes. He put both hands on my upper arms, holding me firmly as he always did when he wanted me to stay present and listen. He looked me in the eyes and continued with ideas about how to make me more comfortable, and suggesting we needed to get upstairs to our guests—and "let's try it again."

I lost it. I pulled out of his arms and backed away from him. "I can't do this anymore. I don't feel safe with him. He scares me and always has. If having sex with her is so important, do it all you want. I'm done. I would rather get divorced than be with these people again."

And then I burst into tears. Sobbing uncontrollably, Drew held me in his arms and said he was sorry, said he didn't realize how hard it was for me. He told me nothing was more important than me and our marriage, and he would never want to risk losing what we had. I'd heard it all before, but hadn't yet become strong enough to see the cycle was beginning again.

We stayed downstairs and talked, and when I was finally calm, we agreed to go upstairs and ask our guests to leave. They were already gone.

I AM Anxious. I AM Lost.

Reflections in the Rearview Mirror:

By ignoring my instincts and feelings, by going along with what my husband wanted to make him happy, I created not only shame but deep resentment, which left me trapped, with my back against the wall.

So often we fail to trust ourselves. People tell us what we want to hear, and even though we know they're lying, we accept it at face value because we don't want to have to take action. We can't see what we can gain; only what we'll lose. The signs are there, but we ignore their meaning.

When *we can't un-see what we've seen, un-know what we know,* we bury it deep until chaos takes over, or we figure out another way. Some of us live in this form of limbo for decades on end.

Despite evidence to the contrary and lacking in self-love, I believed I was nothing without my man. I had placed a high value on being his wife, living in the beautiful house, having nice things and traveling the world, even while I felt undeserving of this stuff and didn't feel like I was enough.

I continued to seek my worthiness from my husband by doing whatever it took to please him, keep him happy and keep him loving me.

What are your "Me, too! Moments" from this section?

Visit www.AnnPeck.com/Me-Too or text ME-TOO to 44-222 to receive your free *Me, too! Moments Manifesto*

Chapter 8

When Two is Not Enough... Am I?

When we're too consumed with what we stand to lose,
we're unable to see our options clearly.
– Ann Peck

After the disastrous ending to our time with the lawman and his wife, Drew backed off from pushing me toward another sexual experience with other people for a while. And then, as usual, his porn use became more frequent until finally, Drew suggested we "try again" and telling me, once again, it would be different this time. Promising me he would take care of me, and if I weren't okay with things, he wouldn't do anything either. Deep down, I knew it was a lie, but I wanted him to be happy. I wanted him to be happy with me, so I agreed. Again, both of us knew the pattern had already been established.

The first couple we met this time around lied about the man's age, which became apparent when we met in person. We saw them a few times, and as nice as they were, and as much as Drew wanted to bed the wife, I didn't have it in me to continue to pretend to be attracted to a man almost twenty-five years my senior. Fortunately, mentioning my lack of attraction to her husband caused the wife to flip out, and we never saw them again.

With another one of the couples we'd gotten to know in *the lifestyle,* Drew, and the other man's wife floated the idea of a threesome. Before entering *the lifestyle,* I had only heard about threesomes, having never participated in one. I was intrigued and willing to explore, particularly as it meant delaying the couple thing. And besides, I had grown to enjoy this woman's company and friendship. I opted for a one-on-one with her, Drew not being present, suggesting that it would allow me to get comfortable with the idea. Drew agreed, and for the first time in our marriage, we slept apart the night I shared our bed with the woman.

I've heard people say that it would be easier to be with another woman because we know what we like, which should translate into knowing how to please our female partner. Well, for me that was not the case. Receiving oral pleasure from this woman was no different than receiving it from a man. I closed my eyes, enjoyed the sensations and forgot the person between my thighs had a vagina. When it was my turn, I found myself with no idea what to do and no desire to continue. Nothing about it made me want to learn or even try. I crumbled, made my way back up to her face, crying and apologizing, admitting I didn't know what to do, and couldn't go on. She understood, comforted me, and with her arms around me, we fell asleep. I wasn't sexually attracted to her, and yet, for the first time in our *lifestyle* experiences, I felt safe. My husband was nowhere nearby and yet, I felt safe, which might have served as a red flag if I had been paying attention to my own needs, rather than pleasing my husband.

The next day, after they had left, Drew wanted to know all the details. I knew he was waiting for me to give the green light for the three of us to share sexual pleasures. As I told him about my experience, his energy shifted. I explained I couldn't give her pleasure, and didn't want to have a threesome with a woman. Ever.

His look alone made it clear to me that *I was not done* having sexual experiences with other people if I intended to stay married. This set my mind in motion.

Knowing I didn't feel safe with the coupled experiences we'd been having, and coming to realize a threesome with another woman wasn't going to work for me, I was desperate for a solution. Finally, after getting up the courage, I talked to Drew about the idea of having another man join us. Would it freak him out? Would he be interested in exploring? I never suggested it would be a substitute for being with other couples, but I secretly hoped it would be the solution that got me away from the other couple dynamic. I needed to be able to control the situation and choose whom I would be sexual with while creating a sense of safety. I felt I had found the answer to satisfying my husband's need to have other people in our sex life, and the more we discussed the idea of bringing in another man, the more intrigued we both became.

Our first threesome was with a man we met through a *lifestyle* website. He was ten years younger than me, which made him considerably younger than my husband. Younger guys have never been my thing, I prefer older men—tall, successful, smart men who I can look up to, who will take care of me in every way. And yet there we were, getting naked with a thirty-something man who lived with roommates and didn't even have a full-time job.

He was kind, tender and an experienced bisexual man, which brought up all sorts of concerns about HIV as well as other diseases. Once he produced a clean bill of health, we were off to the bedroom.

I'd love to be able to say the sex with this younger man rocked my world, but the truth is that I got more enjoyment watching the men together than I did being the center of attention. I'd grown up being told that intimacy between men was wrong, so watching them was both erotic and taboo.

We had a few experiences with this man until I finally suggested we find someone closer to our age. He wasn't my type and the novelty of watching this younger man with Drew had worn off. Drew agreed it was time to find another partner, and I went on a mission to find one who would care about me and see me for more than a sex partner, while still being willing to explore sexually with Drew.

If you're not familiar with *the lifestyle,* you should know that this is not usually the approach. For most people, having an emotional connection is the last thing on their mind, and bisexuality is rarely discussed openly unless the conversation revolves around women. Many couples even have rules about not being with a couple when the man is bisexual or even merely "bi-curious," and not allowing emotional connections with their external sexual partners, which is great in theory and probably necessary if your relationship has any chance of surviving. I had reached the point, however, where I didn't believe my marriage would survive without my participation in *the lifestyle.* Seeking a way to make it possible for me to emotionally survive necessitated me finding us another man who I believed cared about me, and who was willing to participate in a threesome with another man.

A few months later, we connected with a man I had dated before marrying Drew. Even though we hadn't worked out as a couple, I knew this man cared about me. He and I had initially met on the same online dating site where I met Drew, so I went back to this site and changed my profile to reflect my desire to bring a man into my marriage. As I looked up old flames from my dating days, this man saw that I had viewed his profile. He then reached out to me, enthusiastic at the prospect of joining my husband and me, as well as exploring his own curiosity with bisexuality. We promptly made plans to have him over to our home.

Drew came in from the other room to find this man kissing my breasts. He rubbed himself as he announced that the sight of us was the hottest thing he'd ever seen, and we should all go upstairs to the bedroom right then and there. Like an addict desperate for their next fix, Drew was always rushing things when it came to sex, but I needed more time. I was enjoying having this other man, who I trusted, tenderly caress and kiss me. The more he touched me while my husband watched, the less anxious and more comfortable I became, and we eventually moved upstairs to our bedroom, where everyone got undressed. We all began exploring each other's bodies.

I knew I'd found the answer. I didn't leave my body during sex; I felt desired, safe, and I had fun. This was going to be an experience I could repeat; one that satisfied my husband's desires as well.

The three of us enjoyed each other like this on a few more occasions until the other man eventually wanted to be alone with me. Drew was more than willing to let it happen; however, he wanted the man to earn the privilege by taking me shopping, out to an elegant restaurant and a top-notch hotel suite. The whole thing turned into a negotiation that felt like a business deal.

Everything with getting together one-on-one fell apart, and as a result, this man's attitude changed. He went from treating me with respect and gentleness to being crude and unkind. He'd send me text messages calling me whore and slut and using other vulgar language. When confronted with his language, he'd say he didn't mean it; it turned him on, and he thought it turned me on, too. I'd text back, "No, it didn't turn me on at all, and instead, felt demeaning." Of course, he could have brought up Drew's requirement that he trade shopping and dinner to have sex with me, but he didn't. After all, that was the ultimate in demeaning—having your husband attempt to pimp you out for trinkets and a night on the town. Instead, he reduced the number of texts until he finally sent one that pushed me over the edge, and I told him to get lost. With him completely out of the picture, I was once again faced with figuring out how to satisfy my husband while keeping myself feeling safe, secure—and married. I longed to be enough for my husband, and even though I secretly knew I never would be, I continued trying.

We found another man online, who after being with him a couple of times, it became apparent he was much more interested in men than women. So while the men thoroughly enjoyed each other, it became more and more difficult for me to pretend to be enjoying myself. I encouraged Drew to see him without me, and when he wouldn't we decided to move on, although Drew would periodically suggest we reach out and invite the man back. We never did.

Finally, we settled in with another man from my past and enjoyed regular get-togethers two or three times a year. The three of us shared a genuine friendship and affection for each other. Drew would still bring up other couples or bisexual men from time to time, so I knew we'd eventually be going down that road again. Still, the relationship satisfied my husband for the most part.

In between trysts with our new partner, Drew would fulfill his sexual appetite with pornography. I had given up arguing about it and decided it was the lesser of two evils, but it turned out to be as bad for my sense of safety and security as the "swinging" with other partners. And it totally messed with my confidence, especially when he'd leave our bed while I was sleeping to view porn and masturbate. He'd been doing it since we first married, telling me he didn't want to wake me—and that it was okay because he only looked at pictures of women who looked like me.

I never understood why he enjoyed watching other men have sex with me and preferred to masturbate to porn rather than making love to me. Hell, even when we did have sex, it was typically mutual hand jobs. Seemed the only time he wanted to have intercourse was when someone else was watching.

My heart ached as I could no longer avoid the truth: I had turned into my husband's personal porn star.

I AM Undesirable. I AM Inadequate.
I AM Not Enough.

REFLECTIONS IN THE REARVIEW MIRROR:

Being open-minded and exploring sexually with others may sound like fun, something you've gotta try "just once," is one of those things you can do within your relationship because it doesn't hurt anyone. An element of fun or not, *the lifestyle* puts up a lot of roadblocks to intimacy, to feeling loved and safe. And when you combine *the lifestyle* with a partner's sexual addiction, what develops is like an alcoholic who chooses the bottle over the people he or she loves.

I went into *the lifestyle* willingly, by my own choice, ready to experiment. A part of me digs this stuff. It didn't start out as something I did simply to please my man. However, I came to realize, rather quickly, that it wasn't what I was after. The fantasy was a million times better than the reality. It usually is.

Somewhere along the way, I came to believe that I no longer had a choice whether or not to participate in *the lifestyle*. If I wanted to keep my man, my marriage, and my life as I had come to know it intact, I believed I was going to have to play along against my will.

Today I know *we always have a choice*. Always. But sometimes we refuse to see it.

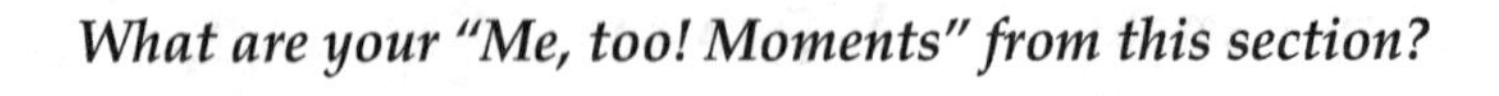

Visit www.AnnPeck.com/Me-Too or text ME-TOO to 44-222 to receive your free *Me, too! Moments Manifesto*

Chapter 9

Viva Las Vegas: Love, Lies, and the Secrets We Keep

To know true love — love of self and love for others, we must stop hiding and extricate ourselves from the shackles of our secret shame.
-Ann Peck

After selling Drew's medical practice, and both of us taking an early retirement, Drew and I spent the summer traveling all over the United States and Canada, including taking a family trip with my son to Yellowstone National Park and Colorado to see my dad. During our travels, we were making new friends and reconnecting with old ones, including Finn and his wife, whom we met during our spring vacation in Jamaica.

A few weeks after getting ourselves settled into our Florida RV community for the winter, Drew dropped me off at the airport for my Las Vegas-bound flight.

The Las Vegas airport and the baggage claim area was huge, filled with people walking between carousels, limo drivers holding up signs, as well as the sort of people one would expect to see only in Las Vegas. There was the drag queen with flawless make-up and curves to die for in a body-hugging neon green dress. A gray-haired couple with matching tropical print shirts carrying old Samsonite® suitcases made before wheels on bags became standard. And of course, the requisite twenty-something girls dressed in too-short, too-tight everything, probably in town to celebrate someone getting married.

I sent Drew a text to let him know that I had arrived safely and would be heading to my hotel, as soon as I found my traveling companion. I looked around, overwhelmed by all of the people and activity. I forced myself to stay calm as I stood there all alone, finally focusing on the exit gate from the international flights. What if the flight was late or worse, canceled? How would I know? What would I do? The reservations weren't even in my name, where would I stay?

I walked around for a while; then decided it best to stay close to my luggage carousel, since my flight and baggage claim area was still posted. It seemed a logical place for us to find one another. As I stood there, I continued scanning the crowd. Then I saw him and our eyes met. He was wearing a crisp white shirt under a navy sports coat, jeans and holding a leather duffle bag. He walked toward me and I toward him. Our smiles getting bigger the closer we got to one another. Until finally, our bodies a mere six inches apart, he dropped his bag, puts his hands on my face, looked into my eyes and told me he'd been watching me from across the room.

"You have?" I said, amazed. Hearing this made me want him even more. It felt like something out of a love story on the big screen, and we were the stars.

"Yes, I have. You are the most beautiful woman I've ever seen." And with that, he pulled me into him and kissed me deeply. I wrapped my arms around his neck. When we stopped kissing, we immediately began talking over one another, saying the same thing.

"I missed you so much. I can't believe we're here."

Finn and I walked hand in hand, talking non-stop all the way to the taxi stand.

Both of us had been to Vegas many times before, in fact, Drew and I had visited two months earlier. And I wanted Finn and me to be able to experience the place without constant reminders of previous trips with our respective partners. Understanding the importance of this, he'd booked us in a hotel neither of us had stayed at before - on the 26th floor.

Finn had suggested Vegas because he could grab a direct flight, and the weather made selling the idea of a guy's golf trip to his jealous wife that much easier. Drew had been instrumental in making this trip possible. He was more than happy to provide an email trail regarding the golf trip he'd supposedly invited Finn to join. He'd included all of the details, like where they would stay, what they'd be doing that Finn would need to convince his wife that he was going to be hanging with the guys non-stop.

I never understood Drew's reason for going to all the trouble to encourage and facilitate my time and a relationship with Finn. Drew called it his "ultimate gift" to me, but deep down it felt like something else was going on, something darker. I used to say he gave me away, but the truth is, it was more like he threw me away. And it wasn't the first time, either. I always suspected he pushed me toward other men in hopes it would create (or continue) a threesome situation, but perhaps it was all about satisfying his sexual addiction through hearing the details. Whatever his reasons, this time it seemed to backfire on him in a big way.

Finn and I had tickets to the early show of Zumanity our first evening, which is a sexually charged Cirque du Soleil production, and an excellent way to relax with one another again. It had been four weeks since we'd been together, and we hadn't had nearly enough time on the phone since then, as Drew and I had spent a large chunk of the time getting ready, then traveling to spend our first winter in Florida at the clothing-optional RV park Drew had found for us.

After the show, we had dinner and caught up. The second show of Zumanity finished up long before we left the restaurant. We talked about everything each of us had been doing since we'd last been together, including my move with the RV to Florida, the crazy community I moved to, and the people who lived there.

Finn always wanted to know how I was feeling about things, no matter how significant or insignificant they might have seemed. We talked about books we'd been reading, our feelings about experiences from our individual pasts, whether from our youth, our former careers or relationships. Both Finn's eye contact and his presence with me when we talked, served as a stark contrast to what I experienced with Drew. Finn paid attention to what I said, how I felt, and what was going on around me. He could anticipate and sense when I needed more time to respond, space to think or even his hand on mine. Unlike Drew who never remembered anything we talked about or did together, Finn remembered everything we'd shared, what I'd said, and what we'd done. He remembered every single detail.

I felt like I mattered when I was with Finn—*which was something I longed to feel with my husband but didn't.*

Walking hand in hand back to our hotel, it felt like we were the only two people in the world.

On our first morning in Las Vegas, we decided to grab a quick bite to eat in the hotel before spending the day wandering around the Vegas Strip. The sidewalks overflowed with tourists and those annoying people that flipped cards at everyone who passed. These cards advertised exotic dancers, clubs, and massages, no doubt with the happy-ending option. People dressed in costumes, like the Statue of Liberty, Superheroes, and dancing girls, even Elmo, were everywhere as they hustled tourists out of their cash in exchange for photos with them. Walking the Strip was like being in another world, complete with the pirates, ships and water at Treasure Island; the outdoor cafe with French music at Paris; and a roller coaster at New York New York.

The more we walked, the more we talked about everything and nothing.

In front of the Bellagio fountains, I taught him all the fun ways I could interact with Siri on my iPhone. "Siri, do you think Finn is sexy?" "Siri, what should we do today?" "Siri, what is your favorite place to visit in Las Vegas?" "Siri, I love you.... Will you marry me?"

At Caesar's Palace, Finn pointed out the work of one of his favorite artists. The fine art photography portrayed the beauty of the major cities and stunning landscapes, in brilliant, colorful images that make you feel as though you are experiencing the location first hand. I entered the picture with Finn as my guide.

That evening, we had dinner reservations at a sexy little place famed for its elegant atmosphere.

Finn wore a black, blue and purple paisley shirt under his sport coat with wool slacks. I slipped into a form-fitting red dress and black peep-toe heels.

We had seen each other fully naked many times before, but seeing each other dressed to impress, knowing what was underneath it all, added to the sexual tension and excitement.

We left our room and enjoyed martinis in our hotel lounge, before taking a taxi to dinner.

Finn knew much of my history with Drew, although we had not yet talked about all of the intimate details of what was happening in my marriage—and in me. Still, he knew enough to know that I was self-conscious.

During our taxi ride, I obsessed over my dress. Was it too short? Too tight? What if it rose up while I was walking? The funny thing is, Drew and I had argued about that very dress when I tried it on at the store. Drew hadn't wanted to purchase it because it had "too much fabric" and now here I was, concerned that it made me look slutty. While Drew pushed more and more to have me dress in less and less, my reluctance grew. Drew enjoyed putting me on display, and the attention we both received was attention he saw as an opening for possible sexual encounters with others. In my mind, covering up was the only way to avoid the unwanted attention. Finn reassured me that I looked beautiful, reminding me that he wouldn't be out with me if he thought I looked slutty.

I appreciated Finn's sensibilities. He didn't have a history of being in the swinger lifestyle, nor the penchant for the activities or manner of dress found there. And I know this seems contrary to how we met—at the nude beach and then having sex at his house without his wife freaking out—but other than one brief experience some ten years earlier, swinging was not something Finn did.

He said I looked classy, and he was right, *even if I didn't see it at the time.*

To help me feel more comfortable walking through the lobby on our way to dinner, Finn put his sports coat over my shoulders. Being naive, I thought doing so would keep people from noticing me. Far from it. As we walked through the lobby holding hands and talking, convinced that I was hiding from the world, everyone seemed to stop what they were doing and focus on us.

I was seen.

That evening, as I walked with Finn, I was considered a beautiful woman, nothing more, nothing less. I wasn't a prize, bait, or something to be had, conquered or traded.

We were seated in the corner of a long cushioned bench. While the others in the restaurant had their dinner partners sitting across from them, we sat so close to one another that our hips touched. We never ran out of things to talk about, and this evening was no exception. Dining on a variety of appetizers, accompanied by a beautiful New Zealand Pinot Noir, Finn began. "I've told you before I don't let many people in. I don't know how you made it past my walls and into my heart, but I'm so glad you did. I love you, Ann, and I'm so grateful to have you in my life."

I confessed my love for him, allowing myself the fantasy of the two of us being together forever. I imagined we could have the life that I had always wanted, the one I thought I was getting with Drew, the one that deep down inside I knew I'd never have with either of them.

When we finally left the restaurant, I was no longer thinking about my dress, only about this man, and my fantasy of a life together.

Even though we were in Vegas, and there was so much to do and see, at my suggestion, we stayed in the next evening, ordering sandwiches from room service. Dressed in only in robes and slippers, we positioned our chairs in front of the floor-to-ceiling windows where we ate dinner and drank wine overlooking the shimmering lights. Our conversation went in all different directions, from the light and laughter-filled to the somber and serious, where we both sobbed. On that beautiful December evening, tucked away in our finely appointed room, overlooking the lights of the Las Vegas Strip, Finn released a secret he'd been carrying around for more than twenty years. It all began when I asked him why he'd never had children.

Finn had grown up with an alcoholic father and a disengaged mother. He'd spent his childhood keeping secrets about what was going on at home, while simultaneously trying to protect his mother, and to win her affection. What he'd wanted more than anything was an emotional connection, which she was utterly incapable of, according to Finn. And here he was, in his fifties, still trying to connect with a woman, on a deeply emotional level, and going about it in all the wrong ways. Exactly like me.

"I recognized early on that I didn't want to bring a child into this world for that kind of existence." He didn't want to be responsible for causing that much pain to another human being. He began to tear up, and his usually perfect posture relaxed as his shoulders dropped and fell forward. "I've never shared this with anyone, not even my wife," he said looking out the window into the night. "I feel so safe with you. I know I can share anything and everything with you." He turned to face me. He told me the story of how he'd gotten his first wife pregnant, and insisted she end the pregnancy for the very reason he'd described. And then, he went on to have an affair with a work colleague, while lying to his wife and pretending everything was normal.

"It feels so good to be able to tell you everything about me, even these things I've been so ashamed of," he said. "I love you, Ann." That marriage had ended painfully in divorce when his wife discovered his affair. It was an experience he wished never to repeat. Even as I heard his words, I believed our situation was different. I mean, he was here with me, in Las Vegas after all. I ignored the fact that I was *at least* the third woman he'd been involved with, and kept secret, since committing to his current wife. I believed my love for him, our love for one another, would be enough to overcome any obstacles.

Less than forty-eight hours later, I was on a flight back home to my husband.

I AM Seen. I AM Delusional.

Reflections in the Rearview Mirror:

We walk the planet with a mindset, a set of beliefs, behaviors, and thought patterns that we have developed over time. When we are *not aware* of them, particularly the destructive varieties, we're destined to repeat our mistakes. These errors are the inevitable consequence of our many blind spots. It's not as simple as being a glutton for punishment; it's that when we've thought and behaved a certain way for so long, these things become hard-wired—*things like keeping secrets and feeling shame.*

Until we are ready to examine our belief systems, our habits, our thoughts, our reality, then make different choices, we'll continue to seek out the familiar. These negative patterns do not go away on their own; they require conscious attention and effort to eradicate them.

I believed that *if I were good enough,* I would win Finn over. I thought that *if I loved him enough,* he would rescue me from my troubles, and I could heal him of his pain. Not once did I examine those things about our circumstances that made us less-than-ideal partners. I heard only what I wanted to hear, saw only what served my desires at that time. I blamed his wife's alcoholism and my husband's addiction, yet believed our actions and love for one another were justified. I even convinced myself our affair was okay because my husband had encouraged us, and his wife hadn't freaked out when we'd first been together at their house.

I believed we could be together forever. I needed to believe it. Finn knew my past and still loved me. I didn't believe anyone one else ever would. My marriage was destroying me, while Finn offered me hope. So I clung to the idea of life with him and ignored the truth of the kind of life it would be. Underneath it all, I knew the truth. *We always know the truth.*

The good news? Wonderful men exist out there. We can have the entire package. Clean up your mindset, learn to love yourself with everything you've got, and he'll be waiting for you. You won't need him, but you may want him. And if you do, you'll feel the difference. I promise.

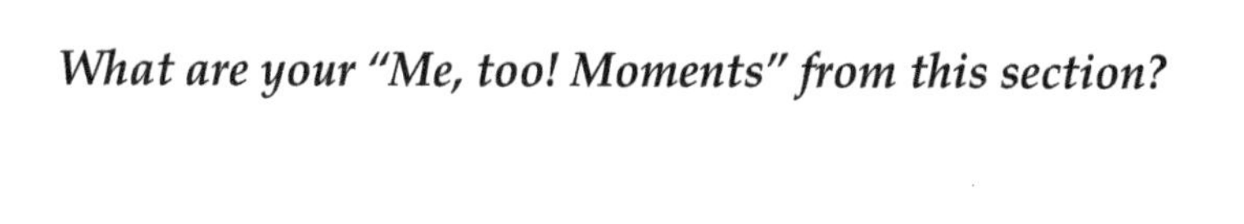

What are your "Me, too! Moments" from this section?

Visit www.AnnPeck.com/Me-Too or text ME-TOO to 44-222 to receive your free *Me, too! Moments Manifesto*

Chapter 10

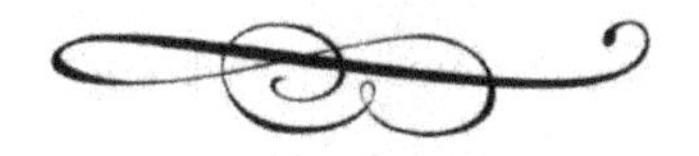

The Puppeteer's Punishment

Courage allows us to see all that we fear,
all that we stand to lose,
and everything that we might gain.
– Ann Peck

After my trip to Las Vegas, Drew and I returned to our home where we spent the holidays with my children and my dad. On Christmas Day, the kids went back to their father's; my dad returned to Colorado, and Drew and I flew back to our RV.

Our RV community was nearly full during the winter months. While some lived there year round, many, like us, had come from the cold north in search of a warm winter. Since declaring my love for Finn, I had finally stood up to Drew, telling him I would no longer be participating in any more coupled *lifestyle* experiences. I said I didn't care what he did—provided he didn't do it in our community or with anyone who lived there. He agreed, yet I sensed he would continue to push me as he had before. It took a few weeks, and once again, it happened.

Drew and I had been partying in the sun all day and didn't feel like cooking. We walked naked around our community, cocktails in hand, stopping to talk to friends along the way. When our next-door neighbors, renters from Canada, suggested we combine our leftovers and have dinner together, we were quick to agree.

Drew started making out with the neighbor's wife while I set the table in our outdoor kitchen, and I pretended like I didn't see it. When he positioned himself next to her, with her husband next to me at the table for dinner, it became impossible to ignore his blatant disregard for our agreement that he *would not get intimate* with someone in our community. Whether with Drew's permission or believing Drew's actions gave him an invitation, the husband from next door reached into my robe to caress my naked breasts. Stunned and not wanting to cause a scene or embarrass this man, I gently and silently removed his hand, and excused myself from the table. Drew was oblivious to what had happened. Nor did he notice when it happened again a few minutes later. I removed the man's hand a second time, backing away from him. I loudly announced to everyone that if they wanted to play, they'd need to go next door since I was going inside to watch television. Our neighbors quickly retreated to their RV, preferring a foursome to a threesome, and Drew came inside, furious with me for ruining his evening.

While Drew ranted on and on about how I had Finn, and how I was now preventing him from having anyone, I asked him why he didn't step in when the neighbor violated me by grabbing my breasts. Twice! I already knew the answer, but I wanted to hear him say it. He didn't. It was no different from when he was having sex with the woman on the deck of the cruise ship in Europe. Then, as now, he didn't see me. He was so caught up in the frenzy of sexual contact with someone other than his wife; he *couldn't* see me. Drew continued to place all the blame on me, and dismissed the fear I felt as a result of his failure to protect me and keep me safe. He refused to sleep in our bed that night, and I knew it was his way of punishing me.

As the weeks went on, we didn't speak of that night again, and Drew continued to encourage and support my relationship with Finn, even as the relationship took me on another supposed "guys only" golf trip (with a cover story from Drew)—this time to Hawaii.

One month later, Drew and I sat in our RV in Florida, discussing the health of our marriage, agreeing it was on shaky ground. He blamed my love for Finn and demanded I end things, while at the same time refusing to commit to a life together without other people. Still believing I could save my marriage by continuing to go along with what Drew wanted, I ended the relationship with Finn. Heartbroken and scared of what my future would entail, I lived with constant anxiety, withdrew into a personal fog, and walked around on eggshells. My use of chemicals increased to numb the pain and block out the reality of how we lived until finally, we decided I'd stay in our home alone for a while, while Drew stayed in our RV.

Drew's email arrived five hours earlier, and I was still feeling numb. I kept playing the words over and over in my mind. "I know in my heart our marriage is over.... I hope we can do this quickly and without lawyers."

Drew wanted a divorce. The initial shock had worn off enough to be able to carry on a conversation with him. "What happens next?" I asked him, trying to hold back the tears. Simply saying the words out loud was making everything real.

"Well, Ann, we're going to need to figure out how to divide things up, so we both have enough to live on."

I burst into tears. I didn't want to be divorced, again! And what kind of impact would this have on my children?

I could excuse the failure of my previous marriage, but this one? I'd put on such a false image, letting family and friends believe we were living a glorious life and were deeply in love. How would I explain this?

I did not want to be divorced again—nor did I want to live the way we'd been living. Most important, *I didn't want to hurt anymore.*

When I'd often replay the story of our life together, it always came out the same way. If we stayed together…

- Nothing would change, except I would lose myself further and further until there was nothing left to recognize as me.

- I would continue to live in a constant state of fear.
- I'd always be nervous, anxious and wondering if the next time he said hi to someone, I'd be expected to have sex with him.
- I would never feel safe.
- I would be accepting the reality that *I was not enough.* Not enough for my husband, and not enough for myself.

If I left, I'd lose financial security. I'd have to find a way to generate income, and even though I'd been able to do it years and years ago, I wasn't sure I knew how anymore. I wasn't sure now, at age forty-seven, I wanted to try again. When we sold his business and retired, it was supposed to be my turn to pursue my interests and my passions, even if they didn't generate income. How could I do that and survive on my own?

It all felt so unfair. If I left, I'd no longer have someone to share my love with, to take care of by loving him. And I'd no longer be taken care of or loved.

If I left, I'd be alone, and I feared no one else would ever want someone like me. Hell, I wasn't sure I wanted myself.

I'd even disclosed the details of our marriage that had led to this moment to Dad, in hopes of sorting things out, and maybe discovering an option I hadn't thought of yet. I'd told Dad everything, absolutely everything. I'd skipped over some of the more racy details, but I'd done my best to share the story of my marriage in an objective way. During the two and a half hours we spent on the phone, I repeated the same mantra. "I feel as though the decision I make right now will set the course for the rest of my life."

As I disclosed the details of how Drew and I had been intimate with other couples even before we were engaged, the truth of our relationship's foundation began to sink in. Only ten days earlier, Drew had told me that my open-mindedness and willingness to play with others was one of the things that attracted him to me. Finn believed, or so he said, that one of the reasons Drew wanted me was to trade me in swinging relationships. I hadn't wanted it to be true, yet the more I told my dad about my marriage, the more accurate I realized it was. I felt sick as I spoke, and my whole body trembled as I revealed both the details and the corresponding emotions. Finally, after sharing as best I could, from both Drew's perspective and mine, I told Dad I had been afraid to say anything to him because I didn't want him to lose respect for me.

"My darling daughter, that could never happen!"

Upon hearing the steadfast firmness of his words, I burst into tears. Sobbing uncontrollably, Dad continued to speak, telling me how much he loved me, how proud he was of me, and how grateful he was that I trusted him enough to share what had been going on in my marriage.

I'd wanted his best advice. I was not looking for him to say what I wanted to hear or to make me feel better.

I'd wanted a solution to my crumbling marriage—and to my profound loss of self.

Dad recommended we leave the community and the sexually charged swinging environment we were living at in Florida. He then started in on all of the things Drew needed to do, including coming back home and getting into counseling. He outlined the possibilities of what might be going on with Drew physically, emotionally, and hormonally.

Finally, I lost it.

"This isn't about Drew, this is about me, Dad. I don't want him to come back. I don't want to live like that anymore, and Drew isn't going to change. He'll say what I want to hear, and when enough time has passed, he'll suggest we try again. It's been like that since the beginning, and it won't change. Drew won't change. I need to."

I told Dad how much I loved him, and hung up.

After seven years of being in this kind of relationship with Drew, I wanted my life back. I wanted me back. I was tired of looking in the mirror and not recognizing the woman I saw there. My once-smiling eyes had gone dull, and I couldn't see anything beautiful about myself. I saw only a scared little plastic Barbie doll without emotions—a thing to be dressed up, put on display to entice the attention of others, a puppet whose every move was choreographed to fulfill the puppeteer's desire.

I was on the outside of my life, looking in.

Although I'd been telling Drew for years I felt as though I'd lost myself, and needed to find myself again, now I was terrified of doing it alone. I was even more terrified of not doing it at all.

Drew cleared his throat; we'd been on the phone for a half an hour, and we started arguing again. According to him, he had simply sent the email to get my attention, but he didn't want a divorce. He didn't need other people and only wanted me.

Something wasn't right with what he was saying. I wanted to believe him—that he wanted me. Only me. I wanted to feel as though I was enough for him.

But as he talked, the tears flowed, and my gut screamed. Everything felt tight. He'd said that same line of BS a million times before, and I'd always believe him. Then, the second I'd finally relax, it would blow up again. He'd push for us to experiment again, and I'd agree. It always ended the same way. The cycle repeated over and over.

This time, I didn't believe I'd survive another cycle.

I believed his email was the final piece of the puzzle necessary to taking back my life, being my own person, and living in a way that made me proud of myself. Thanks to much soul-searching and my conversation with my dad, I had clearly identified the necessity of choosing myself as a priority, and no longer sacrificing my values.

I believed we would find a peaceful and kind method of ending our marriage while continuing to love and support one another, even though heading on different paths. I believed ending our marriage was the only way for me to have a future where I felt safe, secure and ultimately, loved. This was quite odd, since, at that point in time, I was barely beginning to like myself.

An hour in, we were both crying and yelling.

"You're the one who fell in love with another man," Drew screamed at me. "How could you do that to me?"

"Are you kidding, you fixed me up with him! You encouraged us to have a relationship!"

I reminded him I wanted to go to counseling and he'd said no, telling me we didn't need outside help. We could talk things through together.

"You're overreacting, Ann. I've told you; you are the most important thing to me."

The most important *thing* to him.

I reminded him of his response when I'd asked if he was willing to do whatever it would take to rebuild our marriage and stay together. How he'd said, "You mean, are we willing to compromise who we are and what we want in order to stay together." I reminded him how I'd told him I could not live at our place in Florida where the swinging atmosphere permeated everything, and I could no longer have other—or even the option for other—people in our marriage. I reminded him how he'd agreed to my request, only to suggest another threesome with our male partner less than twenty-four hours later. I screamed into the phone, "I can't do it anymore. It's killing me. I can't live on edge all the time, never knowing if you're going to want to bring someone we're just meeting into our bed. I don't feel safe!"

And then he says the words I'd been hearing throughout the previous seven years. "I don't want to lose you. I don't need the option for other people; I want you."

My heart was racing, and my head was throbbing. I wanted to believe him. I always wanted to believe him. Despite Drew's email ending our marriage. Despite telling Dad how I didn't want Drew to return, that I didn't believe Drew would change, and I didn't believe he would forgive me for what he saw as me abandoning him by focusing on Finn. As I talked with my husband on the phone, I wanted to believe him again. I wanted to believe I could have the life we planned to share. I wanted to believe I was enough for Drew and that this time, he meant every word he was saying.

It would be so much easier to believe him, rather than end our marriage.

After ninety emotional minutes on the phone, I was exhausted and on the verge of giving in. Through the throbbing of my head and my gut in terrible knots, I felt my body ready to collapse. And yet, the words that came out of my mouth were not, "I believe you," but rather, "I can't do this anymore. I'll have to talk to you later."

From the early stages of our relationship, we'd had the agreement of being open and exploring with other people. I'd attempted to change the agreement more times than I can remember over the course of all those years, and every single time, I'd let go of what I wanted, what I needed, and agree to continue with what my husband desired. I feared I'd lose everything that mattered, although I'm not sure the fear was conscious. *Everything is always easier to understand in hindsight, especially decision making.*

I never did call Drew back that day. Instead, I spent most of the evening on the phone with a girlfriend. I told her everything and read her drafts of the email to Drew I had spent hours composing. She asked me about money and encouraged me to transfer half our joint money into my personal account. I assured her there was no need, as Drew wanted to take care of things without lawyers, and I trusted he would care for the kids and me while we finalized things. It was well after midnight when we finally hung up, and I clicked send on the email to Drew. Exhausted and emotionally spent, I collapsed into bed.

I woke up the next morning with the same kind of deep, inner knowing I'd had when I realized I'd been raped nearly thirty years earlier at the age of eighteen. I catapulted out of bed and ran breathlessly to my loft office. My mind was racing faster than my fingers could move across the computer's keyboard. Once logged in, everything I already knew deep inside was confirmed. The bank accounts were sitting at zero. Hundreds of thousands of dollars were all gone.

I sat numbly in my chair. I was witnessing, firsthand, what I'd always known, and what I had always feared. In the same way, he'd shut out his first wife, his daughters and his former fiancé; he had now shut me out and cut me off. He'd used his money to control all of us, to show his love—or his hate for all of us. We were all to be punished for not doing what he wanted, when he wanted, in the way he wanted. I'd asked him early on in our relationship, "How do you shut off your emotions for someone you loved so deeply?"

"When I'm done, I'm done!"

I always knew he was capable of it. From the very beginning, I knew, and I'd made many decisions along the way to avoid disappointing or angering him. I'd done things that made me feel ashamed of myself to keep him happy. My husband knew the two things I feared more than anything in the world was *being unloved* and *not having security,* and he used that knowledge to pull me along. And I had allowed it.

I stared at the account screens, showing zero balances, the things I had feared most were now a reality, and I couldn't breathe.

Before I knew what was happening, I found myself huddled under my desk, with my legs at my chest, rocking back and forth as the room went dark.

I AM Alone. I AM Afraid. I AM Courageous.
I AM Resilient.

Reflections in the Rearview Mirror:

When facing life at a crossroads, how often do we take the easy, safe and comfortable path, only to later look back and question our choices? It seems the only time we don't question our decisions in these instances is when we're too busy hiding from the reality of what we've gotten ourselves into.

During my time alone, I came to realize that things were never going to change in my marriage. I was smart enough to recognize that I couldn't change my husband—*I could only change me.* But change is scary, and even after verbalizing the change I had wanted, the change I was willing to make, self-doubt crept in and almost won.

That's how easy it is to stay stuck.

Only with courage can we overcome fear and self-doubt. It was courage that allowed me to go on, even with my worst fears realized. It is courage that will enable you to go on in the face of the same.

In the aftermath, I discovered that I wasn't so much fearful of losing love and financial security, but rather of my inability to handle those things if they happened. I was even more terrified of completely losing myself.

Maybe you feel the same.

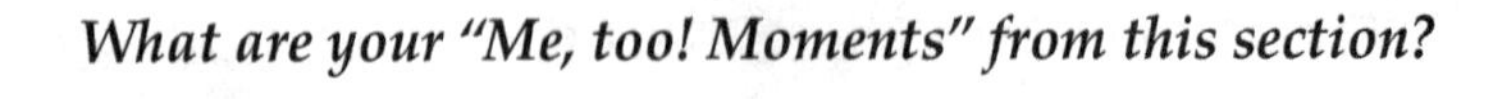

Visit www.AnnPeck.com/Me-Too or text ME-TOO to 44-222 to receive your free *Me, too! Moments Manifesto*

Chapter 11

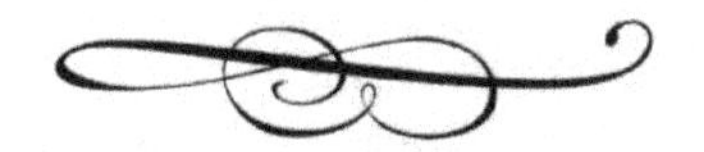

The Gifts of Grief and Moving On

The need to feel significant,
the need to feel as though we matter,
does not make us needy.
– Ann Peck

My divorce from Drew had taken eight months and had been final for almost two months by the time we'd handled all of the paperwork and financial exchanges. I had been living on credit cards and managed to get them paid off while enjoying the bonus of accumulating enough miles to fund a quick spring break trip for my fourteen-year-old son and me.

It was Sunday night, and we had just returned from our trip to Hawaii. My son was already back at his father's when I received the call. My dad's wife was phoning to update me on his declining health. She told me how her daughters, my stepsisters, were making calls, arranging meetings to interview hospice providers, and how all of them had met with a hospice staff a few days earlier. They hadn't signed Dad up with them and would be looking at similar organizations. She was bringing me up to speed…not asking for my opinion.

I began having that old, familiar and unwelcome feeling—as though I didn’t matter again. I'd only been away for a few days, and it's not like my cell phone didn't work in Hawaii, yet no one had thought to call me when my dad, not theirs, reached the point of needing hospice. As they always did, my stepsisters and stepmother were busy doing things that impacted my father, and not bothering to let me know what was going on. After years of dealing with this sort of stuff, I thought I'd accepted it, but knowing Dad's time was limited, I realized not only had I *not* accepted it, all the old feelings were coming back in spades. These were feelings of being replaced, sense of jealousy that he had moved away from me to be near them, feelings of being unlovable. This totally pissed me off, because, logically, I knew it wasn't true, but I couldn't stop the waves of emotion from flooding over me.

The head fog started to consume me. Drew was gone. Finn was gone. My son was back at his father’s, and my nineteen-year-old daughter was living independently. Now my dad was going, and I didn’t matter. They didn’t need me. They didn’t want me; none of them wanted me. I was all alone.

I had struggled with these feelings of what you might call “insignificance,” ever since my dad and his wife had decided to move to Colorado, where her daughters were living. I was nineteen and in college when Dad had announced that they were leaving. He claimed he'd always wanted to live there and yet, my mom claimed she was the one who had always wanted to go, and Dad told her no. Who knows what the truth was, all I knew was Dad was leaving with his wife and would be living near her daughters. I took it personally, as a sign that I wasn't good enough, that I wasn't worthy of him sticking around. Only eighteen months after my rape, which changed how I lived in the world, I took his move as confirmation that I didn't matter and wasn't lovable.

In recent years, I'd come to know how much Dad loved, wanted and needed me, and still, the voices in my head wouldn't shut up. *He's our dad, not yours… You're adopted, he's not your dad anyway… You didn't live with him, so how would you know?... We grew up with him; you didn't… He left you when you were a child… His work always came first… You were never a priority… You got the leftovers of his time… You didn't matter… If you mattered, he would have made you a priority… If you were lovable, he would have given you his time.*

With my stepmother yammering on, those voices were back in full force. The more they talked, the more I wanted to cry. Now, oddly composed, my stepmother had stopped talking, and I said, "Well, it sounds like your daughters have everything taken care of."

I have to tell you; it hurt to hear all that had happened without my input. It hurt to hear that Dad talked to hospice, and none of them had thought enough to let me know. It's as though I'd been replaced as his daughter. Again. Like he didn't need me. Again. Like I didn't matter. Again, all these old feelings felt new again. I told my stepmother as much, not knowing how she would react to my candor.

I could hear Dad in the background asking for the phone. He got on with me, and I could no longer contain my tears. I sobbed as he spoke.

"Ann, my darling daughter, you are not being replaced. You could never be replaced." He went on to explain that he'd asked the girls to help him out because he hadn't wanted to disturb me while I was in Hawaii.

"You are my only family. You and the kids are my only family. I need you, Ann. I need you here. Will you please come and help me?"

Hearing Dad's words made me sob even harder. This man, surrounded by the women I had believed he loved and cared about more than me, was asking for me. He needed me. I could hear the pain in his voice as he realized how hurt I was. Even in his weakened state, he still mustered up *the tone* that tells you he is serious and being completely honest in what he's saying. And he was saying he needed me. He wanted me there, and I was his only family, me and the kids, not them. I was the one he needed, the one he wanted, the one who could help him. The one he *wanted* to help him.

As I felt a warm flood of emotion filling my heart, I sobbed even harder, and this time they were happy tears.

Dad was asleep in his chair when I arrived, and despite how peaceful he looked, I knew he was unconscious most of the time, a sign death was growing near. He looked so frail; his skin was pale and thin. I touched his arm and gently woke him. Seeing me, his nearly blind eyes brightened as a smile stretched wide across his face.

As my dad smiled at me, I flashed back to my mother's final days only two years earlier. In many ways, I had become my mother. Doing my own version of a dog-and-pony show to please the man in my life. Even though I'd left rural Iowa and the small-town mentality, I'd developed the habit of playing small, believing I wasn't worthy, or lovable, until finally, after years of misery and self-destruction, finding the courage *to choose me instead.*

During her final days, as she was reconciling her life, I sat with Mom. She tried to explain, make it up to me, and impart the lessons she wished she had known. *Don't let your dreams die inside you,* she'd said. She left this life with regrets and wanted more for me. I'd sat with her back then and learned so much about her and from her, and about me during her final weeks and days. Now it was time to do the same with Dad.

As I sat with him, he gave me a list of things he wanted me to do while I was there, including taking him to various doctor's appointments, which was usually handled by someone he'd hired through the home care service. What stood out the most on his list was the request for me to go through and clean out his office. Not clean and organize, but clean out, ensuring that everything related to our family history, his career, private papers and mementos were preserved and in my possession. At the same time, he wanted me to confirm all the papers his wife would need would be easily accessible. "You are the only one I trust to do this for me."

Dad was a private person, and even though he'd been married to his wife for almost thirty-eight years, they respected each other's personal space and privacy. When it came to Dad's office, no one did anything in there without his permission—no one except me. I realized that day how Dad had always given me the freedom to be in his office and go through his things. Even as a young girl, when he was CEO of the hospital, he'd always made an effort to include me and to have me feel a part of his personal world. And I was the only one he ever let inside his world in this way. I could see that now.

And with this new understanding, I could feel myself filling up with the love and acceptance that had always been there.

This wasn't going to be my first time going through Dad's office at his request, but I knew it would be my last. This knowledge weighed heavy on me. Realizing I would have the opportunity to go through everything and ask questions along the way was comforting, yet it would eventually be over. During my visit five weeks earlier, Dad had given me two assignments: get their taxes organized, and finalize his funeral plans. Now it was time for the office. The opposite of the nesting that happens shortly before one gives birth to a child; my father wanted my help to pull his nest apart. Dad didn't have to say it; I knew he wouldn't let go of life until his office was finished. I also knew that this was his gift to me, I was being allowed to go through his most-prized and personal possessions along with his private writings. I would see not only his things but him. Dad wanted to be seen, in the same way, I did.

"Dad, this is tough, and I want to talk about hospice. You met with an organization last week but didn't sign on with them. I'm wondering why."

I'd experienced the comfort of having hospice involved at the end of both my mother and stepfather's lives, and I wanted this for Dad, sooner rather than later.

Dad enjoyed the respect of my stepsisters, and as long as he was able to speak, they knew better than to cross him by bad-mouthing me. And I knew that once he was gone, my place in the family would eventually cease to exist. I needed hospice for the support as much as I believed Dad needed their services. I also wanted the buffer of having more people involved, people who knew what was going on, as opposed to the women who were my stepfamily, who preferred to do continuous research and never make a decision, or make one too late to matter.

When I arrived at their house on Wednesday morning, Dad said they had discussed the matter and wanted me to research hospices, to get some folks in to interview. By the next afternoon, we met with one hospice organization that they agreed to use.

It was painful watching Dad slip further and further away, and this difficulty became compounded by the judgments and cruelty from my three stepsisters. Yes, a complete Cinderella story where I was an outsider and always had been.

From the moment Dad had married their mother, they'd been the other women in my father's life. In the beginning, I was excited at the thought of having so many brothers and sisters and imagined how much fun we'd all have together being a big family.

One lesson I've had to learn time and time again in my life is that *reality is rarely as sweet as the fantasy.*

Coming to Dad's home for what appeared to be his final days, handling tasks he trusted to no one else, feeling unwelcome by my step family and being verbally attacked by each of them in one way or another, complicated the matter. I was not going to be allowed what I was after—a final deep bonding with Dad—without a fight.

The attacks started when I let them know a hospice was chosen. They wanted to know who had made the decision, implying that I'd forced the issue when it was our parents who had made the decision together. One of them didn't want to accept their decision, arguing that more research was needed, that she'd been making calls. It had always been a competition with them, for my dad's love. For years, these women had used my dad to make up for what they had missed and felt was lacking from their own father. I'd already helped two parents transition with the help of hospice, and now I had made sure Dad would have the same experience. I knew what I was doing because I had done it before. I didn't need their stupid research, and I didn't have time to waste with their personal dramas and the competition for my dad's love. We were running out of time.

The next day, my oldest stepsister tore into me over the phone for twenty long minutes. She brought up everything she had ever felt about me, going back to my childhood. She told me how I had always been a spoiled little brat, getting everything I'd wanted. She called me weak for being unable to handle stress during my divorce from Drew. She accused me of neglecting my dad by not staying at his house and being there 24/7. She called me "unbelievably selfish" and "pathetic," and accused me of not caring about my dad.

I was in Dad's office during this call, and he was in his bed, a short distance down the hall. I saw what bad blood had done to him a couple of days earlier when a different stepsister laid into me within his earshot, and I vowed not to let him know about this assault.

Dad had shared more than once, how worried he was about what would happen after he was gone. He wanted his wife to be taken care of, and he trusted the youngest stepsister and me to get along and make sure it happened. Even with all the drama over the years, she and I were the closest and had much in common. She was also the closest to Dad of all his stepchildren. We always had a good ability to communicate, even when things were difficult. The oldest and I didn't have much of a relationship, so as she barked at me through the phone, I let her go on and on, and I did my best to respond calmly finally telling her I was no longer going to take her ranting on the phone.

Now, if we had been alone and not dealing with Dad's imminent death, I would have handled it much differently. I would have wanted to bring up the issues she'd had with her father, horrific as they were, and how at nearly sixty years old, maybe she should focus more on herself and healing the crap from her past, rather than focusing on what she doesn't like about me. I would have wanted to talk about the apparent resentment she has for me as a result of my dad being a kind, decent, and loving man. I would have wanted to point out how no matter how much she did, how much she said, she couldn't erase her dad and replace him with mine, and how even if it were possible, my father wouldn't allow it.

You see, during those days of being there with Dad, I was getting stronger and clearer on what mattered to him, learning who mattered and why. I knew he cared about my stepsiblings, even loved some of them, and I also knew at this point, I was his only daughter. I was irreplaceable to him. As my stepmom later said, "You were his bright light."

When I finished Dad's office that night, I went into his bedroom, sat on the bed, took his hand in mine. "I finished it, Dad. Your office is done. Everything they need is organized and easy to find." I was so proud of myself for being able to complete this project for Dad, and fulfill his wishes of seeing that everything and everyone has been taken care of. And I knew he would be proud of me as well, which made me feel loved.

"It's all done?"

"Yes, it's all done." I thanked him for giving me the task. I told him that I'd enjoyed being able to go through everything and talk about it with him.

He seemed pleased.

"I love you, Dad."

"I love you, Ann."

And I knew he meant it. I knew that he had always loved me. He had tried, but it had been difficult for him to parse out his attention between his wife, her children and me. I felt deep compassion for this man who I now realized had spent nearly forty years loving all of us the best way he knew how, and wondering if he had done enough for those who mattered. And at that moment, I felt significant, loved and worthy. My heart felt full as I sat there, holding his hand in mine. I understood the journey he'd been on, and it was a life well-lived, even when challenges seemed in-surmountable and the lessons hard to take.

As I lay in bed that night, nine miles up the road in the peacefulness of my friend's guest bedroom, I didn't know how much more of the drama from my stepfamily I could take while watching Dad slip away. I was alone. I could feel the toll the sadness and anger were taking on my physical body as well as on my soul. I prayed for strength. I prayed for answers. I prayed for an end to the suffering.

The next morning the phone rang. It was my stepmother informing me the ambulance had taken my father to the hospital. During the night, he had had trouble breathing, and he'd asked her to call the paramedics.

"Okay, I'm on my way. I'll let you know what's going on once I get there."

The hospital was thirty minutes away, and I wasn't dressed. Somehow, I managed to throw on clothes, brush my teeth, and arrive at the ER in twenty minutes flat. As I drove, time moved in slow motion, in the same the way we see it in the movies.

I burst into my father's room and found him attended to by five different hospital personnel. I announced loudly that he would not be staying. He would be going home as soon as he was stable. They stared at me, and I realized I hadn't introduced myself.

"I'm his daughter, Ann…" his only daughter, I would find myself repeating to many hospital staff as we worked on the plan and paperwork to get Dad back home. The recognition and respect I received from the hospital staff as Dad's daughter, his only daughter, fed me at a time where I was operating on adrenaline alone.

Those six hours in the hospital with Dad were all ours. We shared precious conversations and quiet moments. Dad trusted me to make sure his wishes were realized, and I did that. I took charge and made things happen. I was in my element, doing what needed to be done for someone I loved. It's something I learned from Dad.

Doing it for myself has been a bigger challenge.

By evening, Dad was back in his favorite room at home, laying in a hospital bed, drinking his favorite beverage, an ice-cold Diet Pepsi, with on-site, round-the-clock nursing care from hospice. The case manager and I agreed to meet back at Dad's house at noon the next day to discuss the plan for his ongoing care.

My phone began ringing early the next morning. It was the social worker saying, "Your father appears to be getting ready to transition."

Dad was resting comfortably with oxygen flowing when I arrived. Looking at him, I knew it wouldn't be long. I went to his bedside, held his hand and let him know I was there. I sat with him for a few minutes and then went to talk with the nurses. They let me know my stepmom was still sleeping and my oldest stepsister was planning to leave work around 11:00 a.m. We agreed to let her wake up her mom when she arrived, and I decided to call her and see if she could come earlier. It was 10:25 a.m.

I told my stepsister we didn't have much time. I didn't know how long, but I thought she had time to get there. As I hung up the phone, I heard the roar of the oxygen tanks. This was not what Dad had wanted. After assuring me it would not cause my father distress or hasten his death, we turned off his oxygen and relaxed into the peace and the sounds of birds outside his window. Dad loved listening to the birds in spring.

I sat with Dad, holding his hand and telling him what an amazing father he had been. I told him how much I had appreciated all our conversations, especially over these past ten months. I told him how much he had taught me, how much I loved him, and how much I would miss him. I promised him we would take care of his wife, and that she would be okay. I told him how much my children loved him, and what a good role model he had been for them. I told him he had raised a strong daughter, and I would take care of things, as he wanted. I told Dad it was okay to let go, and for the final time, I said, "I love you, Dad."

Moments later as I held his hand, Dad took his final breath.

My Dad's gift to me and only me was the gift of sharing his last breath. As he breathed out, I breathed in everything that was beautiful, kind, and generous about him—the things that had always been there that I had come to fully recognize in recent years. I was the little girl he had chosen through adoption before he saw my face, and even though my faith was tested and my confidence lacking about his love for me in the years that followed as I shared him with others, in the end, as in the beginning, he made a choice. He chose me.

I learned more about myself during the last weeks of my father's life than I had in the many years prior. In those final weeks, Dad reminded me how much I mattered, how much I was needed. He helped me see that I was significant, not because of whom I had by my side or what I owned, but because of who I was and how I lived. My father reminded me how much he loved me and *encouraged me to love myself the way he did, without conditions, without judgment.*

When I left my home for Colorado to spend what would turn out to be my father's last week alive, I thought I was going to help him. It turns out, he helped me just as much. In those final days with my father, my faith and confidence were restored, and I came to believe...

I AM Worthy. I AM Strong. I AM Significant.
I AM Loved.

Reflections in the Rearview Mirror:

From my father, I had wanted love and a sense of significance. I had wanted more than what he'd been able to give me when I was a child, and then again after my rape, and that had left me wounded and guilt-ridden. I spent nearly three decades seeking out men who would give me these things, instead.

Throughout my life, I had equated the need to feel significant, to feel like I mattered, with neediness, and I didn't want to feel needy, especially coming out of my marriage to Drew. *Neediness, after all, gets us into trouble.*

I learned that as human beings, we actually *need* these things as surely as we need food, water, and air. We need not only a sense of significance, but certainty and love and connection, growth, and the feeling that we are making a contribution. It's a feeling of belonging, of community. When we don't have these needs met, we shrivel up inside, and try to satisfy them in unhealthy ways.

We all carry around old hurts. What we experienced in our childhood or our younger years, affects how we operate in the world as adults—for good or for bad. Too often, we're afraid to go back to our roots and examine our stories, explore our unmet needs, yet if we do, we can often find something that will help us heal and set us free.

What are your "Me, too! Moments" from this section?

Visit www.AnnPeck.com/Me-Too or text ME-TOO to 44-222 to receive your free *Me, too! Moments Manifesto*

Chapter 12

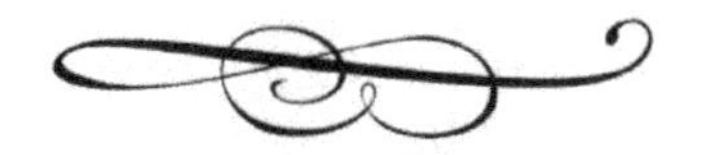

Musings on a Life Half-Lived, and What the Future Holds

How much self-destructive behavior could we steer clear of;
how much shame could we avoid
if we stopped keeping secrets, all of them.
– Ann Peck

Thirty-one years after my rape, I was writing the script for a new keynote presentation and decided to include a shorter version of the rape story. And for the first time, I did not use the words "sexual assault." I made the decision to stop hiding from the truth of what happened, the truth of what I experienced. I rehearsed my speech in front of various audiences, and during one such occasion, a young woman in the audience began sobbing as I told my rape story. After I finished, she privately shared with me how she had also been raped when fourteen by a man in his twenties. She had never told anyone before our conversation that day. Alcohol had been involved, and she had blamed herself, denying it was rape—and denying the impact it had on her until hearing my story.

Over the next several weeks, I let the experience with that young woman sink in. How many rapes could be prevented if I talked about mine? Would more young women make an official report of their rape, if they knew the damage staying silent could cause?

Over the years, I had discovered that being silent did not equate to feeling safe, and I knew this was likely the case for others.

Writing this book offered a similar experience. As I spoke with various women about some of the things I'd lived, I discovered I wasn't the only one. Not only wasn't I the only one who had gone through this stuff, but I also wasn't the only one *not talking* about it. I wasn't the only one living with the silent shame.

And that's when I knew. I knew I needed to write this book and share these stories. I needed to do it for myself...*and for you.*

As a result of my rape experience, I learned I couldn't trust myself. I learned bad things were my fault. I learned there is safety in silence. And it took more than thirty years to realize the lessons I had learned and relied on, were seriously flawed.

By ending the silence around that story, I had the freedom to explore my other secrets. I'd been carrying around other experiences in suitcases of silent shame, fearing what the world would think of me, say about me if I talked about where I'd been or what I'd done.

During my marriage to Jack, I hid my pain behind stuff. From books to office supplies, to the latest trend, whether stamping, scrap booking or candles and home décor, I had them all and they were everywhere. And clothes. I'd go shopping every time I traveled and buy whatever I could find on sale in my size, whether I needed it or not. It's worth noting that "my size" wasn't even my size. I was buying clothes much too big for me, without even realizing it, and I was hiding underneath them, hiding my pain in layers of Ralph Lauren.

When our marriage ended, and I'd lost what mattered most to me—being a full-time mother—I rebelled against everything, calling it "love" of myself and "being my own person." I started speaking publicly about my experience, all while I lied to myself about what was really going on, and went about life as though I was okay. The reality was that my anxiety and depression had taken a hold on me, and I had nowhere to turn. After having my therapy records subpoenaed during my divorce, I no longer felt safe talking to a professional. So I went about my days, smiling on the outside, crying on the inside. And then I met Drew.

I didn't understand sexual compulsion (commonly called sexual addiction) at the time Drew and I were together, and instead, internalized his actions *as something is wrong with me—as proof that I was not enough.* The more I tried to please him, the more problematic my anxiety became. Not only because of how it was impacting me, but also because I had to hide it from

Drew, who thought anxiety and depression were made-up conditions designed to elicit sympathy and attention. He criticized, looked down upon and dismissed those who identified themselves as anxious or depressed. So I spent years hiding these parts of me from him, and myself, while, at the same time those activities were increasing my anxiety.

Hiding in plain sight, even in my marriage. No wonder I lost myself.

When our marriage ended, and I was living alone, my anxiety was at its peak. I was afraid to leave my house, and making a decision felt like pulling my own teeth. It was reminiscent of the anxiety I had after the van incident with Jack, only much worse. I didn't trust myself, and when looking in the mirror, I still didn't recognize myself. I was doing my best to keep it together and didn't even notice how I was falling apart. Three months later, the stress had taken its toll on my body, and I ended up in the hospital.

How blind we become when we don't trust ourselves, when we don't know who we are…

In the same way men gain identity from their work and as "providers," as women, our worth is often found through care-taking and our men. For me, much of my identity has come from the men who have loved me. My sense of self was a reflection of how the man in my life treated me, so it's no wonder I lacked a feeling of worthiness. No surprise self-love was missing.

Conversations with my father, and the stress-induced hospital stay, opened the door to finding love again. They gave me permission to admit I could no longer do it on my own, nor could I rely on a man to give it to me. I had been given a gift—the possibility of living the second half of my life full of love, freedom, and joy. It was time to move on, become my own person, and learn to love myself again…something I hadn't really done since I was a little girl. While the road ahead was scary, it was nothing compared to the road I'd traveled thus far. Now in my late forties, I was ready. Finally.

Writing these stories was gut-wrenching, and it was worse to read them then again later. The first time I shared these words was almost unbearable. This has been my life, and despite the cliché that we wouldn't be who we are if not for our past, a part of me still doesn't want my past to be real. I'd wanted to be normal, the girl next door, a writer, the one who marries the love of her life, has babies and lives happily ever after. I wanted to blend into the crowd.

Reviewing my life up until now, it's definitely not the life I imagined as a little girl, and I wonder: how many of us actually end up living out the dreams our seven-year-old-self creates? More than forty years later, while I'm past having more babies, I still want the dreams that little girl created. Today, I am a writer and as crazy as it may sound given my past, I continue to believe I can still marry the man of my dreams and live happily ever after.

For many of us, our pasts are not pretty, and we've hid them from potential love interests or new friends. We don't want to scare someone away. In looking at my life, it was evident that approach hadn't really worked for me, so I decided to focus on what did work. I took a deep dive into my personal practice with The I AM Habits[1], applying them to all aspects of my life on a daily basis. Then, I decided to be honest about my past early on in new relationships/friendships, rather than wasting time. I knew that female friends, and any man worthy of me, would want to know all of me, even the shitty stuff, and I knew they'd be able to handle it—all of it. Most importantly, I knew any woman or man who I allowed into my life would accept my past without ever using it against me. That was non-negotiable, and over the years, I have said goodbye to many men and women who tossed out criticisms, jabs or passive-aggressive comments stemming from what I'd shared with them—those things I cannot change—things that have been woven into the very fabric of my soul.

I've learned to trust myself, and today I've found a new normal, one where secrets are banned, and shame is released. I've even met an incredible man, the first person I shared my writing with, and he didn't go running for the hills. It isn't easy laying oneself bare, to be completely vulnerable with another. As hard as it has

---

[1] More information on The I AM Habits can be found in the Appendix.

been for me to accept my past, it feels good to be seen, for the real me to be known. It feels good to be accepted and loved for who I am, rather than who someone thinks I am or wants me to be.

Now my goal is to keep moving forward, and not let all the messy stuff from my past spoil my future. Sharing my secrets is the beginning.

I AM Free. I AM Love. I AM Joyous.

Reflections in the Rearview Mirror:

People always want to know what I did to heal, and how I got from where I was to where I am now, but before I share what I've done, I want to emphasize how important it is to keep striving forward. Until we are staring death in the face, our work here on earth is not done. Writing this book and sharing my secrets is a crucial part of my journey because it's about helping others, not just for me. And, before I was able to sit down and write, I had to do a lot of other things first.

I hired a life coach to work with me on business and relationship issues. Okay, that's not entirely true for I had hired this person to work with me, without knowing exactly what I needed to work on, but I knew I couldn't do it alone. Plus I needed help figuring out the business thing. During our second session, we identified relationship issues as a big part of the work ahead of me. Yes, a pretty broad topic, but that's how it started. We met every week for six months and it was worth every penny spent. We dealt with current issues in my business plan and life, while selectively and appropriately pulling in pieces from my past that we needed to address.

If you've never worked with a mentor or coach, it can feel a lot like seeing a therapist, which is why it's important to find one you feel comfortable with and trust. As you search for your own coach, you'll find a myriad to choose from, including those who used to be therapists (or still are), those who received certifications from coach training programs. Many come into the field with life experience, while some (like me) have been practitioners in one or more modalities, such as Emotional Freedom Techniques (EFT) and found coaching to be another name to identify the work they were already doing.

A good mentor will recognize when your needs are outside her or his area of expertise. If that happens, she may refer you on to someone else entirely, or make a recommendation for additional help that still includes seeing her. It's different for everyone. In my case, about six weeks after my hospital stay and four weeks into my work with my coach, I had a breakdown at the beginning of one of my coaching sessions. Two hours after we finished that session, I was sitting in my long-time doctor's office receiving prescriptions for anxiety and depression medications. I've never been one to take pills, previously seeking them when caregiving of my dying mother had pushed me to the brink, and again on the day I discovered that Drew had emptied our bank accounts. So when I showed up that day with an emergency appointment asking for help, my doctor knew things were serious.

I'd love to tell you everything was smooth sailing from that day forward, but I'd be lying. Antidepressants take a while to start working, and the anxiety medication put me to sleep, so I didn't take it consistently. While my coach and I continued to work together, one of her assignments was for me to reach out to friends and let them know what was going on. It wasn't easy. I had become a pro at hiding, and I didn't want people to see me at what I considered my worst. Still, I had made a commitment to my coach and to myself. So on that evening when I found myself in a heap on the floor next to my sofa, crying and wondering why I was even here, rather than taking my own life—which is the direction I was headed that evening—I called a neighbor. She came over immediately, sat with me, comforted me and talked me down from the ledge.

Throughout all of this, I spent time reconnecting with friends and doing my best to maintain the relationships. My anxiety still made it difficult for me to leave my house, but now, rather than hide that fact, I shared what was going on with those closest to me. I asked them to keep inviting me out, and not let me hide forever. Sometimes they even pushed me out the door, which was exactly what I needed. They didn't let me hide and because of that, I became more comfortable leaving on my own.

In the beginning, I thought dating would get my mind off stuff, distract me from the life I had found myself living. I put a profile up online, emailed with a lot of men, talked with some and met a few. It didn't take long to realize the only thing dating did, was distract me from healing myself. I was connecting with men who were no more ready for a relationship than I was. And no surprise, they resembled my former husbands in more ways than one. And I didn't want to see it. As gently as they could, my girlfriends let me know I was in no position to be dating anyone until I got my own shit figured out. I resisted, thinking I knew best, but I couldn't deny they were right. I pulled down my profile and focused *only on me.*

Focusing only on me for a time was one of the smartest things I did!

Without a job, and no alimony from Drew, I had to find a way to support myself. In full denial, I wanted to pretend it was all a nightmare. When that didn't work, I started selling little things and, big things, whatever would give me some cold hard cash. I lived on my credit cards and carried debt for the first time in years. I also went to the local food shelf. I had previously donated to this food shelf, and finding myself on the other side of things was one of the most humbling experiences I have ever faced. Our Thanksgiving dinner came from donations from strangers, and my children's Christmas presents that year came from the generosity of the local Lion's Club.

Fighting through my feelings of low self-worth, with the help of my coach and friends, I analyzed my options for work. I never knew when my anxiety would overwhelm me, turning into unexpected and uncontrollable sobbing or a full-blown panic attack. I feared being in public and having these experiences overtake me. Still, I applied for jobs in retail, and was rejected for being overqualified. They worried I wouldn't stick with the positions if something more suited to me came along. And they were right, except it wasn't about something coming along; it was about *creating the something,*

My work with my coach reinforced my decision to create something that brought me joy and made a difference to others. I believed the gift in all this was the opportunity to pursue my dreams, to turn the second half of my life, into the life I'd always wanted, always dreamed of. I returned to speaking, writing and working one-on-one with women. I went through an extensive sex coach training program and received acceptance into a doctorate program in human sexuality. It's been an uphill climb, filled with roadblocks and disappointments, but I've never given up. I've invested heavily in myself to attend retreats, conferences and trainings, to go through programs and work with mentors and coaches. In the early days, I had no idea where the money would come from as I handed over my credit card, time and time again, to pay the fees, but I believed. I believed it would come in some form or another, and it eventually did.

The speaking, conferences and trainings have taken me all over the world. Yes, I went from being afraid to leave my house, to traveling all over the world. It hasn't been easy, but it has been worth it.

Through my writing, the trainings, travel, and speaking, I've met the most extraordinary people—

people who inspire me, challenge me, and who have become like family. These people and the experiences we have shared led me to starting my podcast, *Straight Talk for a Curvy World®*. This is where I share conversations with people, talking about the things *we don't talk about,* including the secrets they've never spoken about before. My goal on the podcast, as with all my work, including this book, is to remind women: ***you're not alone, you're not the only one and, you're not crazy either!*** You can check out our podcast at www.AnnPeck.com/podcast.

Of course, as you might imagine, in addition to all those things, I've also read lots of books. I share a list of my favorite books, and how they helped me on my website. As a bonus, I even include a list of my favorite songs that have motivated and inspired me along the way. See them all here: www.AnnPeck.com/resources.

Whether songs or books, each one gave me something to grow from and with, yet at www.bonesigharts.com I found the most profound and inspiring words of all:

She could never go back
and make some of the details pretty.
All she could do was move forward
and make the whole beautiful.

-Terri St. Cloud

That's what it really comes down to, my friends. We cannot change our past. What we can do, must do really, is move forward with our eyes, minds, arms, and hearts wide open. And along the way, we must share our stories and release our shame if we ever want to live out our biggest dreams, our deepest desires, and experience the bliss of a life full of freedom, joy, and overflowing love.

The time is now my friends. *There really is no safety in silence.*

Will you join me?

About the Author

Ann Peck is a clinical sexologist and skilled sex and intimacy coach, writer, dynamic keynote speaker and host of the popular *Straight Talk for a Curvy World®* podcast. Ann used to be consumed by anxiety and sexual shame and was afraid to leave her house; now she travels the world writing and speaking about the things we don't talk about – things we hide because of guilt, shame or fear. Ann is a frequent contributor to *Huffington Post,* has been interviewed on shows across the country, and had her work featured in numerous places including: *The Good Men Project, The Coming Out Lounge, and Silence Speaks*. Ann's mission is to help you remember you're not alone, you're not the only one, and you're not crazy either. When she's not traveling or soaking up the salt air from an ocean, you can find her writing and relaxing by a lake. To book Ann for a media appearance, speaking engagement, or to inquire about coaching with Ann, please visit www.AnnPeck.com.

An Invitation

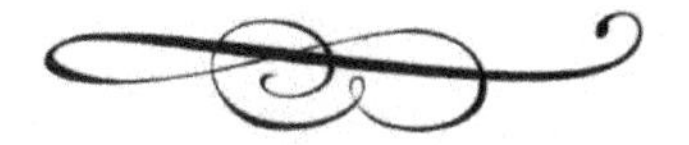

If reading this book had you saying, *Me, too!* Or brought up your own secret shame stories, stories that have kept you *Smiling on the Outside,* you're not alone. Many of our readers have had the same experience, and they discovered that sharing their secrets gave them the freedom, joy, and love they'd been missing.

Even if you're not ready to spill all your secrets, I hope this book has inspired you to believe in second chances (even third, fourth and fifth chances) as well as the power of self-love and the promise of sharing your story with another and hearing the words, *"Me, too!"*

I'd love to have you join *The Me, too! Movement.*

To learn more, please visit www.AnnPeck.com

READER'S GUIDE

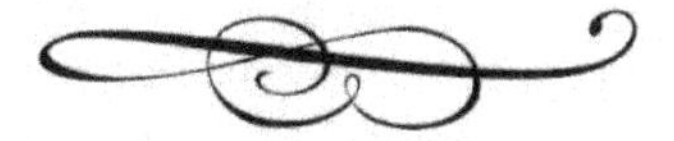

A Conversation with Ann Peck

Curvy World Reader's Circle: Your book gives readers a deeply personal look into your life. As you were writing or even after you finished, did you think about withholding certain stories or the whole book from publication? Did you wonder if simply writing the stories was enough and maybe sharing them wasn't necessary?

Ann Peck: Only about a thousand times! I sobbed through every chapter, and considering the number of chapters and rewrites; it means I pretty much cried every day for more than a year. I thought a lot about quitting during the writing process, and then I'd think about that woman who shared her rape story with me—how she had blamed herself and didn't consider it rape since she'd been drinking—until she heard my story.

I did really hesitate about including the chapters where I talked about my children so much so that they were the last stories I wrote. Once I finished the manuscript and was ready to send it to my editor, I first shared it with the man in my life, my partner. That was hard. Even though he already knew my stories as I told them, it was really hard to know he had read all the details. I wasn't prepared for how I was going to feel at having someone—even someone who loved me—read them. It was then that I started having doubts as to whether I should really publish anything.

And then something beautiful happened. Seriously, when I look back, this was the moment I knew that *to not publish this book would mean I was still hiding,* still keeping secrets. My partner had an incredibly strong reaction to something I had written, and I felt horrible, really horrible, but I couldn't change any of it—not my past nor his pain. I loved him, and not only couldn't I make his pain go away, I was responsible for causing it. I felt helpless. And I realized, my past might be too much for him to handle, and he might walk away, despite our deep love for one another. I knew I had to let him figure it out on his own. And there I was, faced with the possibility of losing love, and for the first time in my life, I knew I'd be alright even if love left. Through his pain, I saw how much I really loved and accepted me, my past, and how important it was to share my stories. It made me love him even more, you know, for giving me that awareness about myself. Such a gift.

CWRC: In addition to the awareness you gained from sharing your words with your partner, what else did you do that has allowed you to love the woman you see in the mirror?

AP: In addition to everything you've already read about, I spent a lot of time figuring out who I was and who I wanted to be. My practice with The I AM Habits was a huge part of this, as I was able to gain terrific clarity on what mattered most. For me, loving my life from the inside out is reflected by how I feel and how I see myself in the mirror, so in addition to my focus on personal growth and learning, I made taking care of my appearance and my health a priority. With the help of some wonderful women in my community, I developed a sense of style, and manner of dress that reflects who I am, not who someone else wants me to be. I also invest in facial treatments, getting my hair and nails done on a regular basis, eating healthy, meditating and exercising.

CWRC: In chapter two, when you're talking about the rape, you mention returning to school, and a teacher you were close to was the only one who knew what had happened. Did she know about the rape?

AP: Yes, she knew. I didn't tell her until she came to see me in the hospital, but by then, she already knew. That's how it was in my small community; everyone knew everything.

CWRC: You don't address it, but this teacher knew about the rape, and she didn't report it either. Why no mention of that?

AP: No, I didn't mention it. In fact, I didn't even make the connection about her not reporting it, and also being a mandatory reporter, until I was in the final editing phase of this book. I had mixed feelings about whether to go back and add in details around that and ultimately decided to leave it the way it was. I'll never know what prevented this woman, my teacher and confidant, from stepping up and speaking out on my behalf.

CWRC: You've told us you don't have memories of the actual rape, which seems like a blessing. Did knowing you had been raped have an impact on your ability to be physically intimate with a man?

AP: Yes, it had a tremendous impact in the months and years that followed. Whenever I found myself getting intimate, my body would react, and I couldn't control it. I'd start shaking, jerking uncontrollably, I'd have a difficult time breathing, and I'd start to shut down. This was how PTSD (Post Traumatic Stress Disorder) showed up in my life – although I had no name for it at the time.

To say it freaked out my partners would be an understatement. I'd end up having to explain what happened, which would result in me sobbing, while he wondered what he'd gotten himself into. In the beginning, I learned to manage my body's response by numbing it with chemicals before getting physical. This calmed my physical reactions, but it didn't stop me from leaving my body during sex and watching from outside myself. That happened almost every time for years afterward, even with the same partner, but I never said anything. It became another one of my precious secrets.

CWRC: You've shared some examples of how your body was giving you signs of being impacted by stress. Do you have other examples you can share?

AP: Yes, and while maybe not a reflection of stress, it was a sign. After I filed for divorce, and before Jack moved out of our house, he would tell me there is no way I had been abused, because I was *"too strong," "too smart."* He had me questioning the experiences I'd had with him, because I had never called the police, and I didn't get broken bones or black eyes. So one day as I doubted myself and what I believed, I made it the focus of my Angel meditation. By the time my meditation was done, I was sobbing (which I do a lot, as you can tell), and I went into the bathroom to blow my nose. As I looked in the mirror, I saw it. The biggest black eye you can imagine—and I'm not talking about mascara because I wasn't wearing any—I'm talking about big, black and blue bruises. As I looked at my reflection, I knew it was the sign I had been asking for during my mediation. To the Angels, I said, "Thank you. I understand," and I did. It was that quick. I no longer doubted myself nor the experiences I'd had. And as soon as I said the words out loud, the black eye faded away. Seriously, it was completely gone.

Then, before marrying Drew, when we were planning our first *lifestyle* experience, I lost my hearing and eyesight (not completely, but it was pretty close.) I had a friend take me to the doctor, but they couldn't find anything wrong. Everything returned to normal a day or two later, but I failed to make the connection between the physical symptoms and what was then going on in my life. Now, I believe it was my body's way of visually showing how I wasn't listening to my inner wisdom, nor seeing what was really going on.

Then, in the final six months of my marriage to Drew, I began having upper arm pain on both sides. This severe pain was in the exact place where Drew would hold me when he wanted me to stay present and listen to him. Again, no medical explanation and the pain didn't respond to over-the-counter medications. And then one day, when Drew wasn't around, I used EFT on it with an affirmation about him and *the lifestyle.* For the first time in months, the pain lessened, and I began noticing a pattern of the pain showing up when Drew was around. Focusing on the emotional connection between the pain, Drew, and *the lifestyle,* using EFT is the only thing that reduced the severity of the pain.

Thanks to EFT, I haven't had the pain since the week Drew emptied our bank accounts.

CWRC: Other than the two chapters when you were with Jack, you don't talk much about your children. Do you have a close relationship with them? How have all these experiences impacted them? Did they know about your lifestyle with Drew?

AP: As I mentioned, I didn't want to write about my children at all, but in the final analysis, I believed the two chapters I included were necessary for the reader to understand the flow of my life, as well as the stories that came before and after. My children are doing well, and we are very close. As to what was happening in my marriage to Drew, no, they were not aware. None of those activities were going on when my children were with us.

CWRC: Let's talk about pornography. It came up in both your marriages. What's most interesting is how Jack was looking at wife swapping websites, and that's exactly what you ended up doing with Drew. By the time you met Drew, were you comfortable with porn?

AP: Wow. Where do I begin? As I wrote, I was not familiar with porn, other than "*Playboy Magazine*," when I was with Jack, so my discovery of what he was looking at completely freaked me out. It's hard to say if I was scared because of the porn itself, or because our relationship was already a mess, and the porn discovery made me feel less safe. Probably the latter. I didn't get curious about porn myself until after Jack and I had separated, and I was exploring the world of online dating. Returning to dating and having sex with new men scared me as I feared a return of the negative body responses I had experienced years earlier. I began exploring my sexuality on my own and having rather explicit conversations with some of the men I met through the dating sites. It was during this time I started viewing porn. A couple of the men I talked to would send me links or subscriptions to their favorite sites, and we'd talk about them. These conversations and the viewing of porn, allowed me to get comfortable with pornography, myself, and my sexuality. It was anonymous and felt safe. I never had anything negative happen as a result. Maybe I was just lucky.

Drew was the first man I dated with whom I shared porn. And as you've read, I blamed porn for having an adverse impact on my self-confidence and my marriage. Still, I'm not against porn at all, as I believe it can be part of an individual or couple's healthy sexual expression.

CWRC: Did porn lead to going to the nude beaches and swinging? Who's idea were those things?

AP: The nude beach was my idea, and didn't come from porn, it came from my love of the ocean and the sun and my desire to experience them uninhibited. There is something so beautiful and freeing about walking naked on the sand while the waves come rolling in. It's not a sexual thing, although many swingers also enjoy the nude beaches.

As to the swinging itself, it seems like the idea first came up as a result of watching something similar in porn. Drew and I were early in dating and both curious. One thing led to another, and there we were, members on a *lifestyle* website looking for potential couples with whom we could explore.

CWRC: When your marriage with Drew ended, you talked about how dating turned out to be a distraction from healing yourself. How soon after your divorce from Jack did you start dating?

AP: I didn't wait long at all, and started dating shortly after Jack moved out. In the beginning, I would justify it to myself as being okay, since I'd known the marriage was over long before he moved out, and I'd seen a counselor. Then, as time went on, I'd justify it because we'd been separated for so long.

I met Drew less than three months after my divorce from Jack was final. I was reeling from my loss of custody when we first met and then when Drew reappeared a while later; I just had the experience with Jack, the children, and the van. I was extremely vulnerable, and the last thing I should have been doing was dating anyone. *I didn't spend any time alone, working on me.* None! But I didn't see it. I didn't want to, so I focused on Drew. All I saw was this handsome, accomplished and well-off man willing to pick up the pieces of my messed-up life. And as you've read, I was one hot mess. I lied to myself and stopped paying attention to anything that would jeopardize the future I wanted. The truth is, I did the same thing with Jack. I mean, with both men, I knew they weren't right for me. I knew…but I lied to myself.

And the real kicker? I *knew* I was lying to myself, and did it anyway! That's how it works when we're searching for love outside ourselves.

CWRC: You write about still believing you can marry the man of your dreams and live happily ever after. Do you really believe that? And how do any of us know when we've found the man of our dreams, and that we're ready and not lying to ourselves again?

AP: Yes, I really believe I'll have my happily ever after with the man of my dreams. As to how we'll know when we find him, I believe we just know these things. It's that little voice inside—our inner wisdom, whispers from Angels, our intuition, whatever you want to call it. We always know. Whether we listen to that knowing is an entirely different question. And I think we are aware we're not lying to ourselves when we're not trying to control an outcome. When we believe we are going to be okay if that love leaves, sad sure, but okay, nonetheless. I believe it's the difference between needing someone else to make us feel whole vs. being whole on our own, and needing the other person in our lives because we want them and love them.

CWRC: What's next for you?

AP: Definitely more books! I'll also be expanding my sex coaching practice in a way that allows me to help even more people release sexual shame and experience the joy of sexual pleasure. This work is a deep passion of mine, as our sexuality is the foundation of our humanness and impacts every single area of our lives from our health, well-being and intimate relationships to job or business performance and financial stability. Readers interested in learning more are invited to reach out to me directly at www.AnnPeck.com.

Questions for Discussion

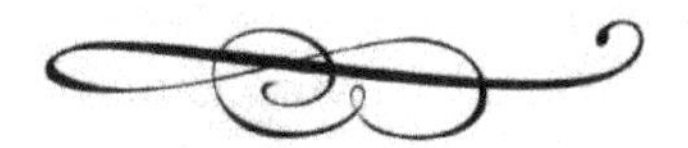

1. Ann's rape took place when she was eighteen and a senior in high school. This is an age where we don't see the long-term consequences of our experiences. Did you have any experiences in your youth that led to long-term consequences you can now recognize?
2. How would you describe your feelings when you read about Ann losing custody of her children?
3. Did reading this book help you identify your own examples of how stress has impacted your physical body and health? Are you still being impacted?
4. Ann writes about her experience on the deck of the boat when Drew was having sex with the stranger, calling it an *emotional rape.* How would you characterize her experience?
5. Were there parts of the book that made you cry? Which ones? Did any make you laugh or get angry?

6. Ann writes, *"When you feel like you don't matter, you start acting like you don't matter."* Are there examples from your life where this is true for you?
7. When you review where you currently are in your life, are you living out the dreams your seven-year-old self-created? If not, do you still believe you can or even want to? Why or why not?
8. Did reading this book bring up your own secret shame? If yes, what will you do now that you've acknowledged it?
9. What is it, if anything, you cannot "un-see" in your life?
10. Whose name would you place in the following blank? ____________________ *really needs to read this book!*
11. Why do they need to read it? Write down what you'd tell them, and then, tell them, when you recommend or gift them a copy of this book.

GRATITUDE

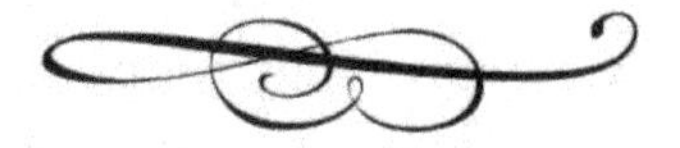

As I am unable to change the past, it is with deep gratitude that I acknowledge this book would look vastly different, if it existed at all, were it not for those four boys, all freshmen in high school, who raped me on that October evening in 1984. My prayer is that through sharing the stories I lived both that night, and as a result, in the years that followed, others may be spared such experiences. And for those of you who are not, for those of you who said, *"Me, too!"* while reading, may you find comfort and healing in knowing: *you're not alone, you're not the only one, and you're not crazy either.*

To Ann Sheybani, my book coach, kindred spirit and treasured friend. Thank you for helping me pull out the stories, even the difficult ones. Without you, this book would look vastly different.

To my editor, Connie Anderson. From the moment we first met, I've loved your no-nonsense, tell-it-like-it-is approach. Working with you on this book has been a joy and a privilege. I am proud to call you friend.

To my interior and cover designer, Ann Aubitz. Your artistic vision turned my manuscript into a real book, while your cover design brought it all to life. You are incredibly talented, a joy to work with and I'm so grateful for our friendship.

To my friends who have been there through it all, sharing stories, laughing, crying, shopping, holding my hand, wiping my tears, pouring the wine and reading earlier versions of this book, thank you.

To my podcast guests who share their secrets and stories with me and our listeners at *Straight Talk for a Curvy World®*, your courage and vulnerability inspires me.

To my clients who trust me to guide them along their own journey of sharing their stories, and to come out from hiding. I am privileged to serve you.

To the friends who have become family through The Summit Mastermind, WOW, PDP, and HPS. Thank you for being a part of the journey.

To my dad, may he rest in peace, for believing in me, respecting me and loving me—when I couldn't do those things for myself. For encouraging a love of books before I could read, and always saying YES, to buying yet another book or sharing one of his own. For helping me to see loving myself as the most important thing I'd ever do. For promising me, if I learned to love myself as he loved me, without conditions and without judgment, I would find a life full of freedom, joy and love. Thank you, Dad, for keeping your promise.

To my mom, may she rest in peace, for encouraging my dream to be a writer, by using a manual typewriter to convert my third grade handwriting into legible text as I created and published my elementary school's first ever newspaper, thus instilling in me a life-long love of the written word. Whose regrets about failing to share her own stories, along with her dying words to not let my dreams die inside me, fueled me to keep going when it would have been far easier to give up. Thank you, Mom, for showing me the way before it was too late.

To my children who were forced to grow up much too fast. Your courage and resilience inspires me every day. I am beyond proud of the beautiful, kind, loving, and compassionate people you are. I love you both to the moon and back again for infinity.

To Erika and Katrina, for always being there for marathon phone calls, late-night texts, wine dates, and pity parties. You've picked me up off the floor, talked me down from the ledge, laughed with me, cried with me, and been voices of reason when I couldn't think straight. You've been strong for me when I had no strength left, and you've always been there to keep me going for the light. I can't imagine doing life without you!

And finally, to D., for understanding the importance of this book, and for pushing me to finish. Thank you for your patience, your undying support, for seeing beyond the stories of my past, and showing up in every way that matters. I love you. xoxo

APPENDIX

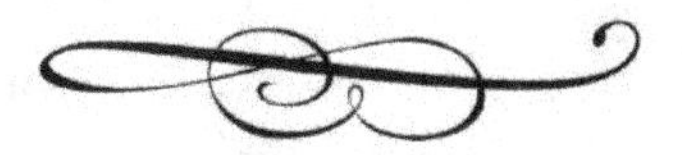

Me, too! Moments

If you saw yourself in any of the chapters of this book, or in the end of chapter ***Reflections in the Rearview Mirror,*** you may use the following questions to begin the process of identifying and releasing your own secrets and coming out from hiding. And if you'd like to go deeper with this work, including eliminating sexual shame and gaining body and sexual confidence, please visit www.AnnPeck.com.

Ask Yourself...

1. What I AM statements have created the person I am today?
2. What am I staying silent about in an effort to avoid the judgment of others?
3. How am I failing to trust myself?
4. Are there any roadblocks in my life that keep me from feeling safe and loved?
5. How does self-doubt prevent me from making changes?

Many of the I AM statements at the end of the chapters were not positive statements. I have since changed them for myself in my own life, and have included the changes here, so you can see how it's done and change your own negative I AM statements into positive ones.

I AM Worthless	**I AM Important**
I AM Weak	**I AM Strong**
I AM Nothing	**I AM Valuable**
I AM Unloveable	**I AM Lovable**
I AM a Bad Mom	**I AM Invincible**
I AM a Failure	**I AM Successful**
I AM Alone	**I AM Connected**
I AM Terrified	**I AM Protected**
I AM Powerless	**I AM Powerful**
I AM Trapped	**I AM Free**
I AM Invisible	**I AM Seen**
I AM Heartbroken	**I AM Healing**
I AM Anxious	**I AM Calm**
I AM Lost	**I AM Purposeful**
I AM Undesirable	**I AM Desired**
I AM Inadequate	**I AM Capable**
I AM Delusional	**I AM Wise**
I AM Afraid	**I AM Courageous**
I AM Not Enough	**I AM Enough**

The I Am Habits

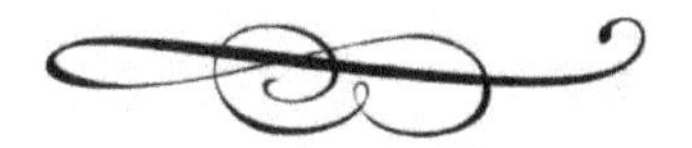

CLARITY
Know who you are, and who you are not.
COMPASSION
Show mercy and understanding first to yourself and then to others.
COURAGE
Come out from hiding and own your story.
CONNECTION
Believe in something bigger than yourself and the people around you.
CREATIVITY
Free your imagination and discover your life's potential.
CURIOSITY
Seek to learn, grow and understand the world.
COMMUNITY
Surround yourself with positive, uplifting and like-minded people.

Resources

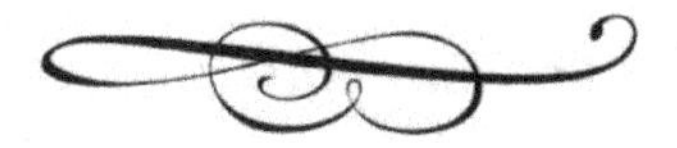

Adult Children of Alcoholics (ACA)
www.adultchildren.org

American Association for Nude Recreation (AANR)
www.aanr.com

Battered Mother's Custody Conference
www.batteredmotherscustodyconference.com

Codependents Anonymous (CODA)
www.coda.org

Minnesota Association for Children's Mental Health (MACMH)
www.macmh.org

National Coalition Against Domestic Violence (NCADV)
www.ncadv.org

National Sexual Assault Hotline
(800) 656-HOPE (4673)

National Sexual Violence Resource Center (NSVRC)
www.nsvrc.org

National Suicide Prevention Hotline
(800) 273-TALK (8255)

CPSIA information can be obtained
at www.ICGtesting.com
Printed in the USA
LVHW032050230223
740259LV00006B/800